What reviewers are saying about *Pra*

"This book is Sofa King magnificent!"
Victor Diamondtuck, "Sofa King" of Vic's House of Places to Sit

"Makes *War and Peace* seem only 1,269 pages long!"
Prof. Nosehair, University of Creeping Vines

"Dude. Dude. Wait....Dude...No, hold it...aw, man...Dude, it's gone."
Jimmy Rastablunt, literary advisor to the J. Edgar Hoover Memorial Hemp Fest

"These essays are the perfect size for bathroom reading."
Frank Weaselpants, Head Chronographer: Flushing Institute

"I was surprised to find the essays are actually funnier than these reviews."
Ellen Leroche, author of *That Wasn't a Crouton*

"Has the ability to drill into local color and beyond. Spoken with a humorous voice, the insights are both poignant and stunningly perceptive."
Paul Turner, President of the Prancing Lavender Bunnies

"Reads as if it was originally written in American English."
Stephanie Duh, director of the film *A Walk Down the Path of the Bloody Obvious*

"It earned him an early release."
Dr. Chance Electrode, Spirit of Insanity Hospital

Prancing Lavender Bunnies and Other Stuff

from the
Darkside of Independent Cinema

Prancing Lavender Bunnies and Other Stuff
from the
Darkside of Independent Cinema

Paul Turner

First paperback edition: December, 2007
Published by Lulu.com in the United States of America
ISBN 978-1-4357-0459-6

Cover design by Megan Beierle
Book design and production by Lainie Turner
Author photograph by Berry Jauer

To order a copy of this book, please visit:
http://www.lulu.com/content/1356764

To receive weekly emails from Paul or learn more about the Darkside Cinema, please visit:
http://www.darksidecinema.com

For Sim

Contents

Introduction

There is a script I want to write. A man gets off a bus in a nondescript small town. He has no money, no name, no past—completely new to the world. As he walks down the sidewalk, he knows he has to do something to make a life for himself. He passes an old theater and stops and looks at its once majestic marquee, fractured neon, and empty poster cases. Across the street is an old motorcycle shop. Its windows covered with dust and tin signs promising speed tarnishing to grey.

If I were to put myself in this script, I would have a hard time choosing between the theater and the motorcycle shop. All things being equal, this wouldn't be an easy decision for me. Do I want to turn a dusty old building back into a place where people come and celebrate life and fiction, or do I want to put my life into orbit around the world of two-wheeled joy that always makes me glad to be alive?

Meanwhile, back in this world, I chose movies. I didn't restore an old palatial cinema. I turned a warehouse and a department store into small movie houses. My motorcycle sits in the garage.

My heart still lives as much in the wind as it does in the projection booth. I derive as much joy in timing the shutter in an old Motiograph AA 35mm projector as I do in sliding a freshly bored cylinder over a new Harley piston. There is as much life in watching someone emerge transformed from an auditorium as there is in sitting by a fire after 500 miles in the saddle, with old friends who don't need to fill the air with conversation. My college philosophy teacher once told me that religion is that thing that makes sense to us. My faith is divided between two entities: The wind and the screen. I feel acutely alive when watching the passing world through my motorcycle windscreen. It's just as nourishing to see the faces of a rapt audience lit by the light reflected from a movie screen.

I'm very lucky to live in one reality and be allowed to write about the other. When I pop open the laptop, the love of movies and motorcycles seem to flow out of my keyboard, combining in some incestuous hybrid of passions. In the cards dealt us, my dual affections are a pair of aces I can play at the table of life.

On September 12th, 1997, the Avalon Cinema opened its doors. After 3578 wonderful, trying, many unforgettable days, Avalon Cinema closed her doors for the final time on June 30th, 2007. Meanwhile, on April 1st, 2005, the Darkside Cinema had opened its doors to the public. The Darkside Cinema riffed its name from the old movie palace across the street, the Whiteside Theater, which closed in 2002 after 80 wonderful, trying, many unforgettable years. The Whiteside is an institution in Corvallis, and building a theater across from her was almost presumptuous. So, we named our theater with a nod toward our neighbor across the street. Some like the name. Some don't.

In the late 1990s, I started sending out a weekly email that included information about the coming week's films and times. As the popularity of the Avalon grew, so did the list of people who wanted to receive the weekly email.

By the time construction started on the Darkside Cinema in 2004, almost 1,000 people were on the email list. I asked the recipients if they wanted me to include a paragraph or two about the progress of the Darkside from time to time. They handed me the stick to beat them with. It took a couple of years, but the one or two informative paragraphs turned into 1,200-word pontifications, which I named "Other Stuff" and positioned at the bottom of the email, after the movie news. There was no set topic, though I did try to loosely tie it to something to do with the theaters or with my love of movies. When the essays were good, subscriptions soared. When I went too far, a few would unsubscribe, but usually this was offset by many more new subscriptions.

What follows are some of my most coherent essays from 2006—the year this Other Stuff column of mine grew wings. And it didn't hurt that I'd married the best copy editor in the world. Lainie polishes away the offensive edges and bad verb tenses with affection. This allows my tough love for my community to reflect in these words. Here are some of those words, in no particular order.

The Darkside Cinema riffed its name from the old movie palace across the street, the Whiteside Theater, which closed in 2002 after 80 wonderful, trying, and unforgettable years. The Whiteside is an institution in Corvallis, and building a theater across from her was almost presumptuous. So, we named our theater with a respectful nod toward our neighbor across the street. Some like the name. Some don't. One of our most popular T-shirts was inspired by a very serious person ambushing me on the sidewalk in front of the theater to complain about the name.

The Prancing Lavender Bunnies

L ong ago, back in the shire, I was leaving the Darkside Cinema. It had been the kind of day that would send most people to the rooftop with a high-powered rifle, so I was not in the mood to be stopped on the street. But she seemed like a nice lady, so I put on my polite face and listened to what she had to say. That was my mistake. She launched into an ethereal diatribe about how naming the Darkside Cinema the Darkside Cinema was bringing bad, negative energy into the downtown area. I politely explained that the name is a nod to the Whiteside Theater, across the street from us. She was deaf to my explanation and went off on a rather awful new age sermon.

I took it for as long as I could, then my mouth opened—sans blurt filter— and this came out: "You know, you're right. To counteract that negative energy, I'm gonna form a biker gang. Rather than wearing black leather and drinking beer, we're gonna wear purple leathers and blow kisses at people as we ride by. I think I'll call my gang the Prancing Lavender Bunnies. Happy now?"

Without a word, she spun on her heels and walked away. It was almost as if she thought I was making fun of her. When I recounted this story in my weekly email newsletter, I received many requests to join this rather unique biker gang. And so was born the Prancing Lavender Bunnies T-shirt.

If I ever see that lady again, I'll give her a free PLB T-shirt.

The Avalon/Darkside Cinemas have been a major sponsor of the da Vinci Days festival for years. This was our first shot at doing Rocky Horror Picture Show as a fundraiser for the Festival. We were certain all manner of disaster was going to befall us. We got off lucky. For many people, this was their first foray into the insanity that is a Rocky Horror event—because it is always more than just a picture show.

New Year's Eve

It would be safe to say our New Years Eve bash/benefit for da Vinci Days was a hit. Quite a few people showed up and over half of them had never seen DR. STRANGELOVE before. So, their introduction to one of Kubrick's finest was on the big screen instead of the TV at home. After a brief intermission, we carried on with ROCKY HORROR PICTURE SHOW. We did a brief description of how annoyed I'd be if toast, rice, glitter, toilet paper, or anything else hit my screen. The partiers were so good! All things were thrown up in the air, and not toward my precious yet already character-ridden screen. The film left the screen about two minutes before midnight. My two favorite quotes of the evening were:

1. When a customer was told we don't have butter for our popcorn because I can't eat it anymore, she said, "Dude, go on Lipitor. I want my butter."

2. A great line from a chilly customer: "Can you turn up the heat in there? I just had a boob job and my nipples are killing me."

It would be safe to say that New Year's Eve was one of the worst nights at the Darkside in quite a while. For those of you blissfully removed from the weather, let me just say it was raining so hard that confused animals were walking down the street in pairs, lining up in front of Noah's Bagels.

The night started with one of our projectionists effecting a repair of one of the sound processors. Bad news: the repair shut down the processor and blew a fuse in another piece of equipment. Being the veritable projection wizard I am, we had sound again before the end of the second preview. Damn, I'm smooth. But, not smooth enough to wrangle the rain-induced power fluctuations. Sweet Cherry Nut Log.

The first one blew the projector bulb in auditorium one. No biggie. After a 10-minute cool down, I swapped out the bulb and got the show back on the screen. The thing I missed, however, is that the bulb in auditorium two was also shut off. People were coming out and saying, "Uh, we have no picture." Duh, thinks me, why do you think I'm changing the bulb? These safety glasses are not much of a fashion statement and this light strapped to my forehead isn't to practice gynecology. Well, being the clueless, arrogant twit I can be on occasion, I didn't realize they meant the *other* auditorium. Merde.

The good news is, that bulb didn't blow. The bad news is, it took me 15 minutes to re-strike it. In the immortal words of Lloyd Bridges in AIRPLANE, "Looks like I picked a bad week to stop sniffing glue." For those who lived through this night with us, thanks for being so cool. For those of you who went into ultra-dick mode, yep, that would've pissed me off, too.

Often there is more hope than substance. I refused to let the Avalon die without trying everything I could. This piece was written before I pulled out the last of my ammo and dug in for the Avalon's Last Stand. For nine months I remodeled and repurposed the Avalon, pouring effort and money into the hope that she would survive. This made it possible to put the Avalon behind me when the time came in 2007, knowing we'd tried our best.

The Avalon Closes Temporarily

With no ceremony, the Avalon Cinema closed last Saturday. Now, now—it's probably not closed for good, but it will be down for a while. Saturday we had a rather major malfunction, and replacing the part would have cost more than the place has grossed in the last two months. So, we're gonna shut her down long enough to get the bills caught up and do some long-waiting repairs. I know you'll miss the "Avalon Baptism" you get every time it rains. Just be glad we're not Baptists...that would mean full immersion...not just getting sprinkled...never mind...

Whatever happens, it's gonna be different. The last few months we've been trying the discount theater thing, with no success at all. We are looking at all manner of possibilities: beer and wine, live performers, various film series (like bad biker movies week followed by Clint Eastwood movies week, and so on), stupid pet tricks, a shooting range, me hosting a live nightly talk show, psychic readings (how many people knew I was going to say that?), or perhaps penguin tapioca wrestling. Or maybe all of these things. Who knows?

The opening of the local 12-plex started the hammering of coffin nails into the Avalon. Then, Ninth Street Cinemas, in an attempt to keep treading water, decided to start harvesting the art market in Corvallis—the market I'd been cultivating for the previous seven years. Since they had more seats than us, they were able to get the films. These were the films I counted on to pay the bills at the Avalon.

The Avalon really started circling the bowl when the Darkside opened. People love variety, and the Darkside has it times four. Our poor little art cinema was left out in the cold and started to wither. Nights when we had 150 people at the Darkside, we'd have seven at the Avalon. Since we know that alternative cinema in Corvallis will be well represented at the Darkside by the same deranged minds that brought you the Avalon, the writing was pretty much on the wall.

There are times when I would rather write about motorcycling than movies. Often I have to start with a motorcycle story to segue into something more relevant to my movie-going readers. Sometimes that transition is more transparent than others.

Bug in the Eye

One day, a long time ago, when blackberry was a ubiquitous fruit-bearing vine rather than a communication center for your pocket, I was riding an old Harley across the Willamette valley floor. With no warning, a deer decided to cross the road a hundred or so cubits in front of me. Those of us with a little vehicular experience with deer know that where there is one, there is a party. So, I began the rather convoluted process of ratcheting down the speed of this ancient iron hog, revving the engine to line up transmission syncros and intermittently pulsing the front and rear brakes—all while tickling and teasing the gear box down to first gear. As I scanned the roadside for quadrupeds, a six-ped hit my windshield. Insect impact is not a terribly novel occurrence on a motorcycle, doncha know, but this one hit the edge of the windshield and dispersed its exoskeleton into the air. The bad news for me was that my head was turned, scanning for potential venison, thus the shards of bug slipped behind my glasses and lodged in my eye. Well, now.

I wobbled over to the side of the road using my one good eye. Necessity being a mother, I used a pair of nail cutters and the mirror of my motorcycle to remove bug parts from my cornea. It reminded me that life is not a Gump-esque box of chocolates. In fact, life is a burrito full of jalapeños. What you eat now will haunt you later that evening with a burning vengeance. Whoa, my sweet Lady of Perpetual Motion. That evening my eyeball said, Howdy, and thanks for the bug parts.

What the heck does this have to do with anything? Well, disassembling the Avalon is just as painful as extracting entomological armor from my eye. It seems I remember every screw and nail I drove in, over eight years ago. I know it's like cutting off a finger to save an arm, but, man—there is a lot of history in that auditorium. (No, not just on the sofa; you know who you are…) I can work for about three hours and then it's like a wave of nostalgia knocks me over and I just have to get away. It's like listening to your kid scream when she's getting a shot—you know she needs it and it's a good thing, but, damn, you'd do almost anything to make it all better.

With each nail I pull, I can still hear the laughter thundering in the floorboards from MY BIG FAT GREEK WEDDING. As I undo the strings of the screen, I see the jaw-dropping expanse of WINGED MIGRATION. With each curtain that comes down, I feel the emotional tug of CINEMA PARADISO. I know that redoing the Avalon is the best chance to save her, but it is no fun. I had no idea what I was getting into when I opened those doors September 12th 1997. Do you remember what the first movie was?

And the emotional jalapeños burn like a mother every time I walk back into the Avalon and see her torn up. I have to take a deep breath and pick up the crowbar and start dispensing the medicine that goes down hard, but will hopefully bring the Avalon Cinema back up.

Okay, some days I just need to whine like I'm the only one who has workdays that suck so hard the trees are leaning in my direction from the vacuum. There are times when I'm better at letting go of the idea that I have control over the way things go. This was not one of those days.

Fridays

F ridays are rapidly becoming my least favorite day of the week. Since, unlike in some other cultures, our calendar has no sense of humor, we seem to be averaging about one Friday every seven days, give or take. Then again, I guess we could blame pirates, rather than the calendar, for the general suckage of Fridays. Not the pirates who speak using only the consonant "R," but the ones who leak copies of movies out to the world before they are officially in DVD release.

Back when I was learning the ins and outs of this funny business, we traveled to Portland each week to pick up our films from this place in called "The Film Depot." Every print of every film came to us through this magical place. Translation: We knew where our prints were going to be, and we knew who the last person was to handle them. Double translation: We knew *when* we would get our prints, and the last projectionist to run the film was accountable for the *condition* of the print when it got to the depot. Well, thanks to fear of pirates ("Arrrrrrrr!") getting their hooks on our films, the single-digit IQ guys at the film studios decided we needed to hold the movies in our possession for as little time as possible, because the film might get pirated if left lounging in our projection booths. So, now we are not supposed to pick up the movie until the day of the first day of the run. This means that the print often arrives minutes before, and sometimes days after, the first show of the day. Then, they want the print back the minute it comes off the screen, and sometimes sooner.

To accomplish this shuffling of prints, movie companies use various couriers. Now, the actual folks who drop the prints at our doors are usually pretty good folks; however, their handlers tend to occupy the lower end of the evolutionary scale. You could make a drinking game out of the predictability of the excuses they provide when the print is actually not even in the same state as the theater where it's supposed to be played.

"The previous theater missed the pick-up." One shot of cheap whiskey.

"There's some real weather happening there." One shot if it's summer and the pick-up was supposed to happen below the 45th parallel. Two shots if it's spring and they're talking about Tucson, AZ.

"The studio never contacted us." One shot if the studio swears they did contact the service. Two shots if the studio told you yesterday that they did clear it for delivery. Three shots if it's not even coming from a studio.

You can kill the whole bottle if the person at the other end of the help line suddenly launches into some non-Latin based language, mid-sentence—and claims to never have ever spoken English.

As you can tell, all this convoluted print moving has resulted in the complete elimination of movie piracy. It's true, no more do they sell bootlegged copies of movies still playing in theaters on the street corners of almost every American city with a population greater than four. Certainly there is no place on the Internet where one can find a copy of a movie not yet in DVD. Pride can't begin to describe the feeling I get from knowing I'm part of the piracy solution.

Which leads me nicely into last Friday. This week I'm gonna have you help me write the story of the weekly disaster. Circle the one that works best for you.

Last Friday it was:
    A) Raining so hard you needed scuba gear to walk to the mailbox.
    B) Still the day arriving right after Thursday.
    C) The first day of my new diet consisting of pain pills and Sweet Cherry Nut Logs.

The movie we were supposed to be playing that evening was:
    A) Lost on a life raft in the Pacific Ocean.

B) Floating down the Willamette River toward Corvallis, until the delivery service figured out the Willamette flows *north* from Corvallis toward Portland.

C) Used as an emergency rope to lower passengers down from a derailed train on a trestle.

When the print arrived, it:

A) Looked like BROKEBACK MOUNTAIN after Pat Robertson had edited it.

B) Was so late we could only build up the first two reels before starting the show.

C) Turned out to be a Chinese language version of DUDE, WHERE'S MY CAR? with Swahili subtitles.

Once we got it on the screen:

A) The customers released the snack bar people they were holding as hostages until the film started.

B) The projectionist ran bottomless through the auditorium while doing the chicken dance.

C) The clouds parted, a shaft of light beamed from above, the choir sang an ascending C note, and the rest of the night went off without a hitch.

Thanks for playing!

It was a lot of work conforming to the body of regulation that was constantly nipping at my heels during the construction of the Darkside. Some of it made sense, like: no barbeque pits in the restrooms. Some of it didn't make sense, like: not being allowed to raise the floors of the projection booth to accommodate the projectors. This resulted in a really shitty solution that involved using periscopes. Hey, it got us open.

Re-Sounding

I spend a lot of time whining about all the silly stuff I have to go through to keep the projectors spinning. And, frankly, it's too bad if you're tired of hearing it. It will probably get a lot worse before it gets better. I mean, my whining.

I have to admit a certain satisfaction when a fellow theater owner—one who perhaps had a budget to equip their projection booth, rather than just a pile of gears and rollers, lots of stupid optimism, and the love of Jesus in their hearts—calls up and asks for help with a technical problem. As I pity them appropriately, no small part of me is thinking, "Thank God I am not the only one to have refunded a show this week…"

Petty? Hell, yes.

Human? 'Fraid so.

Would they think that about me? I'd be disappointed if they didn't.

For reasons that baffle most experts, when I built the Darkside I was not allowed to raise the floor in the projection booth to get the projectors above the heads of the people sitting in the auditoriums, expecting to see a show. Being the clever lad I am, I built periscopes to raise the beam over the heads of most folks. They were done with first-surface, laser-quality mirrors that were mounted and positioned with the care of laparoscopic surgeon.

Those in the know, know gravity sucks. On the other hand, most plastic surgeons would be out of business without it. Combine time and gravity, and things go downhill fast. (Get it? Time and gravity…downhill fast… Sorry.) Well, our mirrors were acquiring a wee bit of a droop, making it as hard to focus as it is to miss shooting a lawyer in the face with vice-presidential bird-shot. So, in auditoriums two and three, we have eliminated the mirrors and now have a stunning image on the screen. Auditorium one should be done early next week.

I would love to brag about the new sound systems in two and three, but they've been nothing but a huge pain since they went in. They sound great, right up until they don't. Then you hear me using short sentences made up of four-letter words, loud enough to be heard in all the auditoriums, right through the sound-proof walls. Yes, for the price of a ticket, you get to see part of a movie *and* hear about the incestuous habits and other unkind but colorful depictions of Dolby products. One of the many services we offer.

There was a time in the history of the Avalon when I woke up one day and realized I didn't have to go into the booth that day to re-solder something or change out a component. Holy flapping butt-cheeks, Batman, do I really need that day to come *way* soon to the Darkside. More importantly, *you* probably want that day to come soon, too. I'm working all the time to get it here sooner. Thanks for sticking with me.

The devil is in the details. When something is taken for granted, it is often the very thing that causes a problem. What makes it particularly difficult to figure out is that, often, decades have passed without so much as a blip—which takes it off the diagnostic radar. Sometimes it's the very thing that is supposed to help you that ends up hindering.

Sound Problems

Some of you may have noticed the sound in auditorium three has been, well, sucky. In an attempt to solve that problem, I had the technician come in and replace much of it and upgrade the reader. Worked well, then, well, not so much. So we replaced the sound processor. We went from a I-Can't-Believe-It's-Not-Dolby to an honest-to-God Dolby processor. Still sounded like hell. What was worse, the problem came and went, so it was like chasing a greased rat through a slippery sewer pipe. Next, we swapped out a notoriously problematic power supply. That was easy—and useless. What we did next wasn't easy. We replaced the 110-pound sound head that sits seven feet up. So we basically replaced the whole system—some parts of it twice. My work here is done, thinks me. Hah! God said.

I'm sitting at home, having my wife peel me a grape while fanning me with ostrich feathers, and my cell rings. Rather than waiting, I decide to launch into the bad language right away:

"W@#%&%%&*@#???"

"Uh, Paul. Sorry to bother you at home on your night off."

"*&%$%$!"

"I know, but I've got the volume all the way up and people are complaining."

"#$%%$%^&!!!"

"I tried that. It's fine."

"!"

"Okay, I'm going behind the sound rack. Whoa! It just got louder!"

"!!!?"

"I have no idea what I did!"

So, let's review: we changed out the sound processor twice. Installed a newer, better sound reader. Hefted a big-ass cast-iron piece of equipment into place, which killed my back. And the sound still, quite frankly, when it good and damned well felt like it, sucked. Then, my big-footed projectionist steps behind the rack and clears up the problem. Know what the problem was? After all the time, pain, and expense, you know what the problem was? The damn earphones I use to monitor sound had developed a short! For 20 years I have clipped these very earphones to dozens of different speaker leads in as many theaters, and after two decades, they finally died. So, this specter of intermittent sound problems has now been linked to, yep, the times I had the earphones clipped to that processor. The devil is in the details. Boy howdy.

Nothing is ever as easy as it looks. I tend to be a little too worried about the longevity of things I build. This has two effects. One, it takes for bloody ever for me to get something built. Two, it takes for bloody ever to get something I built torn apart.

I Have a Habit of Overbuilding Stuff

T o get the inclined floor out of the Avalon involved 12-ton car jacks, 4-foot crowbars, and the possibility of a future hernia surgery (no, really). I was glad for my engineering excess when I found myself standing on top of the center speaker behind the screen. You see, it's about eight feet up in the air, and the pile of fractured lumber with claws of bent nails would have been my landing pad if I hadn't used a handful of 3" screws to secure the speaker to the cleat on the wall.

So here I am, on top of the speaker, undoing the final screws that hold the screen frame upright. Did I mention the screen frame is made of steel and weighs as much as a 1950s-era American car? Well, that would be an exaggeration, but a mighty small exaggeration compared to some I tell. The idea was to unlatch the frame and let it fall onto the pile of lumber. As the Makita whirred and spun, the final screw came out of the bracket... and I had a thought: I might have secured the frame to the speaker upon which I was standing. Holy hygiene-challenged hyenas, Batman, this could get ugly!

Then time stood still. I had a moment of clarity, just enough time to ask myself what led me to be standing on top of this speaker, getting ready to jump for the cross-beam about three feet above me if those cables I ignored drag down my perch with the screen?

It was all my mom's fault.

You see, when I was nine years old, I asked my mom how movies were made. She handed me an 8mm Bell & Howell movie camera and a roll of film. It went downhill from there. I wanted to watch movies all the time—any movie—and then go out and see if I could make my own version. I had lassoed every kid in the neighborhood to act, and used every dime I could find in the paper machines or earn collecting cans from the beaches of Santa Cruz to buy film and processing. My friend Anthony and I filmed a lot of stop-action stuff with teddy bears and GI Joes. We even did one with GI Joe and my friend's sister's Barbie. His mother confiscated it shortly after its debut. When I become famous, it will show up on eBay. Don't bid until the final few seconds.

When I got out of high school, where did I go to work? A drive-in movie theater, of course! This was a real 'nad pumper for me because it combined cars *and* movies. My best friend Ron and I lived underneath the screen tower and ran the shows. After the shows we hopped in our matching 1960s red Impala Super Sports (and, miraculously, we both *still* have those same cars!) and practiced safe, courteous driving—never exceeding the speed limit or compelling others with similarly appointed vehicles to some sort of competition. Ever. Honest.

Sure I went to college. Did a lot of other things. But always landed back in a projection booth watching light dance through film, at 24 frames per second. So I caved. I decided I needed to be in a theater more than I needed to be anywhere else. Ho hum. All thanks to my mom.

I'm sure if my mom saw me standing on top of that speaker wondering just how this screen falling thing was going to play out, she would have asked, in her best French-Canadian accent, what the hell I thought I was doing. A valid question, eh? She had a certain pronunciation of my name that swapped the vowels (that Ron can still imitate perfectly), which reduced me to about eight years old. Though my mom stopped catching me doing stupid stuff years ago (some suggest it's due to her passing away), at that moment, I could hear her calling, "Puuuaaawwwl!"

There was no blaming this one on my little brother.

Slowly the steel frame of the screen started giving in to gravity, moving away from me, past the point of no return. I grabbed the beam over my head and was ready to grapple onto it if my four square feet of MDF decided to chase the screen to the floor. (I can imagine the cell call as I hang from the beam: "Hi, honey. How's work? Say, could you come on down to the Avalon… no, nothing's wrong… just hanging around, that's all…")

Insert your favorite onomatopoeia here for the sound of a heavy-ass screen hitting the ground.

Evidently I did *not* secure the screen to the speaker. Once I was safely on the floor, I looked at the screen and tried not to think of all the films that had splashed across its white expanse. It seemed a crudely unceremonious way for a screen holding over 30 years (from two theaters) of film luminescence to end its career.

Though I did keep my promise and it did see ROCKY HORROR PICTURE SHOW as one of its last shows (I'm still finding glitter and rice). With any luck, a new screen will start its life in the Avalon in a while. Releasing myself from the soggy sentimentality that binds me to the old Avalon will help the rise of the new Avalon.

Sentimentality is a silly habit that makes things harder than they need to be.

"Puuuaaawwwl, don't be silly."

Yeah, mom. I'm working on it.

Like the marquee reads, Stay Tuned.

This essay proves that there can be more than one genre of problem per week. Sometimes the technical setbacks can combine with the booking hell of competing with two huge theaters just a couple miles away. Then, as if there wasn't enough zest already, the minority of moviegoers wants to make decisions for the majority.

Sound Fix

After a couple months of trying to figure out what the heck was going on with the sound in auditorium three, I did the total un-guy thing and brought in the technician. We were so frustrated after a couple of hours, we were using language that made the hair removal scene in 40 YEAR OLD VIRGIN sound like a Mormon missionary spiel. Then we changed out a huge chunk of the system. It's much better now. And our language got much better.

Which leads me to my next point: we need your feedback. If there is a problem, stop being polite and come out and tell us. Most of the time it's a three-second adjustment. Do you hear a rumble in the sound? Usually that means a bad splice went through and we slipped a couple of frames—this can be fixed in a few seconds. Too, quiet? Too loud? Out of focus? Hey, you gave us your hard-earned money. You don't deserve to sit through that! Oh, and by the way. If you say something *after* the show is over, there is nothing we can do. Funny, that...

You might have noticed we were not the first to get BROKEBACK MOUNTAIN. We are waiting to get a print of it eventually, so it *is* coming. A big Avalon/Darkside thanks to those who said they would wait until we get it. If, for some reason, the Wombat of Bad Luck descends upon us and we can't get a print, I will give you a heads up.

Another point I'd like to make about BROKEBACK MOUNTAIN: I've heard every variation of this title I care to. I understand people not remembering the name and calling it the "gay cowboy movie," but, for the love of bat guano, spare me the spoonerisms, play on words, and the thinly veiled homophobia (believe it or not, there are some regulars who indulge in this). Remember how I threatened to add another $6.50 to the admission if you tell me you're a student of life? I'm about to do that if you miss-name BROKEBACK MOUNTAIN. Because, making fun of this movie is so gay...

Another issue that came up that I wanted to bounce off you is the matter of previews. I was politely informed by a concerned mother who came to see PRIDE & PREJUDICE that she did not appreciate her 13-year-old having to sit through previews for the "gay cowboy movie" and BREAKFAST ON PLUTO. Now, she obviously was a little unclear on the concept of the Avalon/Darkside experience. But, have any of you folks had issues with previews before films? Feel free to share.

First Anniversary of the Darkside Cinema, April 2006

C an you believe it's been over a year since we opened the Darkside Cinema? Well, actually it's been 13 months, which isn't a year. So, if you didn't believe it was a year, you were right. Good for you. So I'm one month late. Sue me.

The Darkside name was conceived on a napkin in a restaurant about three years ago. We had a few other names before we settled on the Darkside. First it was the Denny's Cinema. Then we realized you shouldn't conceive anything on a printed napkin in a 24-hour restaurant. Next, we considered the "Brown O" Movie House…only to discover we were looking at the coaster under my coffee cup. A-1 Theater, Heinz Plaza, Thank You For Coming Cinema, and Wash Hands Before Returning To Work Multiplex were all theater names we considered and discarded pretty quickly. Then we thought, well heck, we're right across the street from the Whiteside. What would be a spiffy way to differentiate ourselves from that grand old gal yet acknowledge her importance, too? We thought about the Gottschalk's-side, the Homo-side (killer name), and the Ironside (wheelchair accessible). Then the Musak played something from Pink Floyd, and the rest is history.

The best part of this whole Darkside experience has been the people. You. That's right, you. You know who you are. The folks who stopped me on the street and thanked me for doing this. Those of you who showed up for the painting party. The Illuminati who enlightened me with their spare swag lamps for the lobby. The individuals who took a chance and lent me money. The list goes on. It did start to dawn on me that many of you thought I was tragically insane and were just being nice to me. "Oh, it's another email from that nut-job Avalon guy. This time he wants lamps. The poor dear. Let's see what we have banging around in the garage."

The worst part of the Darkside construction was a certain incompetent contractor who used bullying and lying rather than just getting the damn job done. My wife won't let me say who it is, but let me know if you're thinking of having some work done and I'll suggest whom you might avoid. What is particularly upsetting is that every other contractor absolutely and totally rocked. I mean, aside from the one ass-hat, everyone who worked on the job was like a gift from the gods.

And we have come a long way since we opened, baby. We started with the projection periscope system from hell. First-surface mirrors did a fuzzy job of getting the image from the projector up to the porthole and out to the screen. Focusing accurately was about as likely as Stephen Colbert being invited to another White House Press Correspondent's Dinner. Know what happens when you spend a lot of money on crossovers for the speakers rather than doing it the cap-n-coil method of old? You spend almost a year trying to figure out why the sound goes from great to downright sucky in minutes. So, the sound has made great strides as well as the picture.

And we ain't done.

We're getting ready to re-seat auditorium three. Auditorium four will eventually be film (rather than digital as it is now) when we get the Avalon reopened. I'm getting hearing-assist devices for auditorium two and working out a deal for digital sound in auditorium one. Hell, we might even get around to painting the entrance!

So this is my chance to say, with no sarcasm or snideness: Thank you. Thanks for coming down and seeing films in our place. Thanks for not coming after me with axe handles and torches when things broke. Thanks for not taking me seriously when I was having a perfectly lousy day and might not have been as affable as I usually am. In exchange, I'll keep rollin' 'em if you keep watchin' 'em.

You can tell by this essay that I was in the clutches of depression over the decline in economic viability of independent theaters. Was I right? Time will tell.

The Death of Cinema

The end is near. Soon all theaters will be closed. Cardboard signs in their windows, made from the boxes of home theater units, will read: **WE GIVE UP**. You will be able to watch the tumbleweeds roll across the multiplex parking lot with a live web cam. You will have your grandson on your knee and tell him stories of the times before we had the 100-terabyte iMovie thingie, "We actually had to sit in auditoriums with people *we didn't know*. Sometimes we even laughed and cried together. Sometimes it went completely dark, and we had to sit there until a human person turned up the lights and fixed the film...yes, film!" You will snicker to yourself at the wide-eyed look of amazement on the kid's face...

The supposed latest nail in the coffin of the cinematic experience was when five major studios announced that you can now download a movie from the Internet the same day it goes to DVD. Prices are roughly comparable to DVDs: $20 to $30 for new releases, $10 to $16 for catalog titles.

And from those who have been at this a while you'll hear…crickets. Perhaps a little yawning. Someone may crack their knuckles and ask, "That all ya got?"

You see, this all started a long time ago. TV was supposed to have killed the movies back in 1931 when there were 40,000 TVs in all of the US of A (9,000 in New York alone). The cinema industry didn't really worry about it too much until the early '50s when CinemaScope, the wide-screen format, was introduced. Thousands of drive-in movies theaters built an extra expanse of screen to accommodate the larger format. If you see a drive-in built before 1953, you'll see newer construction that added more space to the screen, if it's the original screen.

In 1973 HBO started broadcasting movies with no commercials. Once again, the choir was singing the swan song of the cinema.

Yawn.

About that time VHS kicked Beta's smaller, better-looking butt and one could finally watch porn in the privacy of their home. Very quickly people learned to defeat the anti-recording tab on the Disney videos so they could record their porn on innocent looking tapes—which tended to produce an uncomfortable moment when grandma slapped SNOW WHITE into the VCR to appease the rug rats. "Well, kiddies. Sometimes it takes more than a kiss to wake up Snow White. Now, go play outside."

And on it goes: the Internet, DVDs, downloads, earthquakes, floods, pestilence…any of which will spell the end to movies playing in theaters.

Bullshit.

You go to the movies to get the heck outta the house. Yes, at home you can pause the movie to pee. You can also listen to the phone ring (God help you if your phone rings in one of my theaters), the dog bark, the kids unfurl their list of things the world owes them, and you can even listen to the neighbors watching porn on their Betamax. Of course, popcorn is cheaper if you buy it and make it yourself. Probably better for you, too. But, Orville Redenbacher can put that stupid little bowtie somewhere corn won't grow if he tells you his stuff tastes like real theater popcorn.

Movies are actually a great deal. Especially at the Darkside. Come in on any Wednesday, which is Cheap Nite. It costs $10 for you and your date to get in (and if you are a FlickClique member it's only $4 admission for *any* night). If you each get a small popcorn and a drink (both of which are refillable), you can add another $10. So for a Jackson (or less) you can spend two hours with your sweetie and, best of all, not have to talk to them!

If you go out to dinner instead, do you think you're going to get away for less than twice that? And you have to *talk*. Make conversation. Before the food comes this really sucks, because your blood sugar is low. I'm enough of an antisocial bozo with a good meal under my belt. Imagine me pretending I care of about your list of things you think the world owes you—which you insist on telling me about because *your* blood sugar is low.

The cinema experience will be around for a long time. Even when things don't go the way they should in the projection booth, you're still out of your house, hangin' out with other people, and not thinking about work, the leaking car, that hangnail, the war in Iraq, and that exquisite loaf the dog left under the dining room table.

Try ignoring that stuff at home. Much easier to not think about all that with a popcorn in your hand, a movie on the screen, and the faint rumblings of me in the booth cussing at the equipment.

Corvallis is a small town. Some people think we still have wooden sidewalks and outdoor plumbing. Since the studios from which I get my movies are in places like New York and L.A., their attitude can get a little thick. This is where a booker comes in handy. Roger booked movies for me for eight years, through the thick and thin of independent cinema in Corvallis. Booking for multiple theaters gave him an edge. If he didn't like how the studio was playing, he could pull the product from multiple theaters rather than just one. When he took us on, it was a bit of a long shot whether we would survive. Here we are a decade later. Seems like his bet paid off.

My Booker, Not Bookie

My film booker and I have developed a unique relationship over the seven years we've been putting up with each other. When I talk to other theater owners who ask whom I suggest as a booker, I pause before recommending my guy. He's very good at what he does and has stood beside me when most others would have shown me the door. But, he gets mad. At me. He tends to be a little blunt and frequently expresses exasperation at booking decisions that I insist on. The good news is, he also puts up with me when I throw a fit about this movie company or that film rent. I don't like being yelled at or being told to play a movie "because it'll pay off later." Can't say it rates up there with a 20-minute orgasm. But it is part of who he is, and he's worth the mutual drama.

When Roger sent me an email telling me to "put down the tools and market these movies," I initially reacted the way I might react if someone said, "I'm gonna get fit-shaced drunk and try to knock that soup can off the top of your head with live grenades." My response might end with, "…and the horse you rode in on."

Tools are to me what rum is to a pirate, sarcasm is to a teenager, or a grenade pin is to someone with a soup can on their head: really damned important. One doesn't tell me to put down my tools, thank you very much.

My wife and I live in a part of town where working on the car in one's driveway isn't the norm. Since none of my neighbors would groove on me working on my car in their driveways, I tend to do it in my own. I have an affinity for big motorcycles and old diesel Mercedes—double happiness for my neighbors: noise and smoke! (The reality is, we all get along quite well. If I'm under a 300TD swapping out a CV joint, one or more of my neighbors usually wanders over to talk movies or cars.) So this how I blow my days off when Oregon weather dissuades two-wheel recreation—oil changes on the Harleys or chasing rust with primer on my old Mercedes. My darling wife, who cares as much for my automotive ramblings as I do about the price of organic tomatoes, listens politely as I regale her with tales of repaired window regulators and injector timing.

So when Roger, who knows me and knows I'm transforming the Avalon, has the stones to tell me to "put down my tools," maybe I better listen. What that means is, you better listen, too. We have some good stuff coming, so focus your cinematic lust on these coming titles, and if you see my booker, tell him you can't get me to shut up about these films. Please. I'm begging you.

There is an odd muscle memory when it comes to running old theaters. I've been doing it so long, there is very little that takes a lot of thought. I've been through divorces, drunks, deaths, and demonic possession, which left me mentally disconnected from the material world. But, my body knew how to run a movie projector, pour a soda, and make popcorn. No matter how bad it got, I could always thread a movie machine or fix it if something went south. When I visit an old theater like the Fox in Dallas, I can feel the presence of those who share the same ease—who rattled around those 80 year-old walls. Some things have not changed much about the Fox's old projection booth. It's still a steel and concrete box, built to protect the rest of the building from the old nitrate film that could flash and burn faster than 24 frames per second. And don't forget to check out the prominent and undignified booth toilet without a door—a leftover from the nitrate era—that was supposed to keep the projectionist from leaving the booth during their shift. Try enforcing that in a modern multiplex.

The Fox Theater in Dallas

From time to time I find myself running my friend's first-run theater in Dallas. This is not a fate worse than death. Actually, it's not even as bad as conservative talk radio, though it's probably not as good as a Parisian vacation with a stolen credit card and a stated goal to gain 30 pounds.

The mention of Paris isn't total coincidence and/or because I couldn't come up with a better segue. The fact is, I am running the Fox Theater in Dallas as I write this on Tuesday evening, and the movie is THE DAVINCI CODE— a movie that starts out in Paris. The book was not high literature, but at least it had the courtesy to not take itself too seriously. Giving the movie to Ron Howard to direct resulted in the predicted Opie-fication. Even the chick from AMELIE couldn't shake the blandness off of this one. Holy Declining Box-office Grosses, Batman.

On the rare occasion that I see a first-run film someplace that isn't the Dallas Fox Theater, it is usually at some atrocious multiplex. That *is* as bad as conservative talk radio. But this place is way different. First off, it's old. Like *way* old. It's been running since God's beard went white. The coatroom was originally a toga room. (Okay, that's a lie. Because, back then, the natives here did not wear togas. They wore plaid loincloths, tanned from the hides of the roaming Giant Plaid Beasts. But, I digress…) The 235 seat auditorium has painted walls, with stuff actually painted on them. Art stuff. It has art deco light fixtures…tanned from roaming Giant Decos. Frankly, I like it.

It has subwoofers. Ribcage rattling bass swells up from the digital sound system. I can't do this at the Darkside because it would be unkind to the bookstore to knock books off the racks every time a car chase ends with the expected collision, or a flatulent mastodon eats Mexican food for lunch. But, when you have a movie as lame as THE DAVINCI CODE, you need to keep the audiences' fillings dancing in their teeth with some bass, or snoring will ensue.

The Fox has really cool inclined floors. They run all the way down to the screen. I'm 45 years old, and I still wanna run down them. Plus, the aisles are lined with runway lights. Yes, I've been caught a few times with my arms out, running down the aisles, coming in for a landing. I've stopped doing it during full houses with a show on the screen, however. It was part of my sentencing…

They have butter for their popcorn. Since I have to watch my cholesterol I can't have butter on my popcorn, so no one gets it at the Darkside. But at the Fox you can run your cholesterol up to four digits if you like.

They have a real, live box office! This outdoor appendage is a glass-block beauty where someone will sell you a ticket before you enter the building. It even has one of those ticket machines that spits the ticket out at you. They still have to do the math in their heads, though.

So, I like being here on occasion. I actually used to work here before I had a gut and enough debt to crush a non-cocaine-producing country. Sometimes it's fun to go back in time…a long time ago, when Giant Plaid Beasts roamed the earth. You should check it out sometime. Just follow Highway 99 North from Corvallis, up the road about 35 or 40 minutes into Dallas. Look for the sweet little, old-fashioned Fox movie theater located on the town square. And, please—ask for extra butter.

As land values increase, many of the old drive-in theaters are becoming retail spaces and suburban homes. I started my projectionist career at the Woodburn Drive-In Theater, which was, oddly enough, in Woodburn, Oregon. It is now a Safeway and a Starbucks. And I say thank God. Thank God for one more grocery store, and, obviously, you can't have too many Charbucks. As of this writing, the Motor-Vu Drive-in Theater in Dallas, one of Oregon's few remaining outdoor screens, is still in operation. No one knows how long it will be until our culture trades in the few remaining speaker posts for half-caf soy vente with a double shot of caramel.

The Motor Vu Drive-In Theater

The Dallas Motor Vu Drive-In theater opened this last weekend to the glorious Oregon spring time weather: yeah, it rained. But, we are Oregonians! We are tough, as long as there is whipped cream on our mochas, we can wear our Birkenstocks, and our salad is organic. ("I spilled my mocha on my Birkies while reaching for the raspberry vinaigrette for my spinach salad! What merciful god would allow that to happen?!?") We are not about to let a little rain spoil our fun.

I've been peripherally involved with the Motor Vu for a couple of decades now, and have watched it go from a lawless passion pit where life was cheap and the snack bar was not, to the family-oriented experience it is today. The sound used to come to your car via the cast-aluminum rattle boxes that passed as speakers. The sound resembled the emasculation of a hyena mixed with a jackhammer running in a subway tunnel…during a hurricane…with your head inside a watermelon…with someone using a belt sander on it… But, I digress. These days the sound comes to you via your car stereo, in stereo. You tune your radio to the right station, set your seat back, and enjoy. Lainie and I watched

ICE AGE 2 last week, because I think Scrat is the funniest thing on the screen since Clint Eastwood singing in PAINT YOUR WAGON ("Who gives a damn, we're on our way!!!"), and the neighboring car's subwoofers compensated nicely for my rather bass-less Blaupunkt. It was actually pretty fun.

I was working at a drive-in when radio sound hit. People had trouble making their single-speaker analog radios work, and we were doing everything from hanging wires from their antennas to wrapping them with aluminum foil (the antennas, that is) to bring in the signal. Once we even hired a local witch doctor to come out and do a radio dance around cars that didn't have digital locks on their tuners. He was generally as successful as we were with the foil and wire.

The radio waves were transmitted through the old speaker wires in the ground, so every time a speaker post got mowed down by someone trying to navigate their land yacht in the dark, the wires got broken, and from that point outward all sound to cars ceased. Today, most of the wiring lies out of harm's way a foot or two underground. With everything from MP3 players to fashionable underwear sporting FM receivers, getting the sound is no longer a problem.

Then there is the Motor Vu screen. It's huge. It stands so high, the local control tower flies planes *around* it. Okay, not really. But, it is the biggest drive-in screen in Oregon. It's pretty cool seeing an image that big. Let's face it, kids. The clock is ticking on this American anachronism. Soon property values will be too high. We're counting down the remaining summer nights of sitting in lawn chairs beside your vehicle, or in your sofa in the pick-up bed, or in the back of your van on the futon mattress, along with 500 other movie watchers (big-assed van!). These drive-ins will be gone—turned into strip malls with seven Starbucks in a row and a Lackluster Video nearby, so you can rent movies to watch on your pathetic glass screen, instead of on this majestic, 60-foot, white monolith.

We didn't mind the rain that night. The van was warm and the intermittent wiper setting was perfect. We wrapped up in the blanket and laughed as that scrappy little acorn-chasing rodent got chased by cracks in the ice. I'm old enough to have seen PAINT YOUR WAGON at the Santa Cruz Drive-In when it was first released (1969), so this is home for me. Lainie was grateful it was cold enough to keep me from springing out of the car every few minutes to run to the projection booth to adjust something.

We figured out drinking wouldn't save the Avalon and finally closed her at the end of June, 2007. If I really want to depress myself, I can look at all the effort and time put into bringing beer and wine to the Avalon. The other side of that coin is that if I hadn't tried so hard, I never would have forgiven myself. So, here is a look into the process that was the last, best shot at keeping the Avalon as part of Corvallis.

Drinking

I don't drink. It's kind of a recent thing. It actually has to do with health reasons rather than some court-ordered mandate I received for busting up a hotel room, in a tequila-driven rage (though I once kicked the heck out of a plastic trash can after a beer and a half). So, I don't really have an attitude about it. When I'm at a party and someone overhears me refuse a drink, it usually ends up with them asking if I'm a "Friend of Bill's." To which I respond, "I use a Mac. I have as little to do with Bill Gates as possible." Then I'm informed they meant Bill W. By then they have usually surmised I am not an AAer. Even in Canada, I'm not an AA, eh-er, don't you know? Though here I do belong to AAA. In Canada, it's the AAA, eh? I'll stop now.

So, I find myself involved in the paperwork of getting a liquor license for the Avalon Cinema. There is an oddness to this—hawking something to you, my customers, that I can't play with anymore. It seems to be causing some anxiety. It's upsetting my sleep.

Most of us have had the dream about being naked in school. Mine is a different version (hope you were sitting down). I go up on a ladder to change the marquee. I carefully put up: MUSICAL DOUBLE FEATURE: WIZARD OF OZ. SOUND OF MUSIC. When I climb down and look at my work, it reads BESTIALITY DOUBLE FEATURE: HAPPINESS IS A WARM PUPPY. HEAVY PETTING ZOO. I quickly run up the ladder and change it back to the musical. When I get back down, it again reads as the bad, bad one. So I run up the ladder to change it back. Meanwhile a crowd is forming wondering what I'm on (and where they can score some). Every time I change the marquee, it goes back to the bad, bad one. The people get madder and madder, and no one believes I didn't really do it. I dream these things when I try to process the process of getting the beer and wine license. I swore I would never do it—sell alcohol. But here I am, waiting for the final piece of paper to submit the stack of forms to the OLCC, dreaming of naked marquees.

Times change. Things are much different than they were even a year ago in this business. As corny as this may seem, I take seriously the responsibility of bringing independent films to Corvallis. I mean—who else would you want doing it? So, my particular, silly sober preferences have to take a back seat to the reality of what I do. Along with your continued support, beer and wine at the Avalon should help keep both places afloat. Which leads to a smooth and tactful segue: I know the weather is nice and all, but your part in having cool film in Corvallis is to support the theater, rain or *shine*. Get on down here and see a movie or I'm going to drag my landlord, Book Bin Bob, to each of your houses so you can explain to him why I'm not making rent. Because it's a trade: if I have to sell drugs (alcohol) to keep independent cinema in Corvallis, you have to come see the movies. If not, you can count on some pretty colorful double features.

Someone once told me dyslexia is an invisible handicap. Bite me. Bite me twice. There's something uncomfortable about calling a disorder a handicap when I consider it merely a pain in the ass. Whatever the case, I have trouble giving directions to my house, or taking them. Some days there are two lefts. Did you know that? Spelling? Not so gud. Numbers? Who says there is a "right" order? But, I keep on keeping on. Okay, it drove my mom so nuts she joined D.A.M: Mothers Against Dyslexia.

Dyslexia

H ave you ever awakened in the morning and had an octopus on your chest? The worst part is, they cannot sit still, so you have tentacles squirming all over and sometimes they are staring at you with that big eye.

This really has nothing to do with what I'm writing about today, but I always wanted to start a story that way.

Dyslexia is my friend. So that means I get to tell jokes that start like this: "Two dyslexics walk into a bra…"

Six years of college English and I still spell at an eighth-grade level. That is no joke when I have to put the right letters in the right order on the theater marquee. It is embarrassingly unhandy when I misspell a word up there, for all the world to see. The fun part is, most marquee letters don't have an indicator to tell if they are pointing in the correct direction. I literally have to look twice at a "B" or a "D" to remember which way they go. I have to try it in both directions and pick the one that "feels" best. Most of the time I do pretty well. Sometimes I get a call from one of our workers who just passed by the building on the way to their real job. "Hey, Paul. Dude, take a look at the marquee when you get to work, man."

Anyone who deals with this word-wrecking mind-twist knows there are ways to get around it and make it work. Back when I ran theaters for other people, I had to call in ticket numbers every night. It became very common for my boss to call back: "So, how did you get over 900 people into a 200-seat theater? You must have transposed a couple numbers." Ya think?

I cannot see the difference between certain numbers that are next to each other—somewhat cumbersome when it comes to balancing a checkbook. I recently found a stack of legal pads that I used to use to track all my checks. I'd write down the check and the amount and then later *call* the bank's recording so I could *hear* if the checks had cleared—because if I looked at a statement, I often saw the wrong check number. I had to hear it in order to make sure it was right.

So how did I get through high school, you might ask? Cheating, mostly. I pasted the spelling words in 720-point type to the front of the teacher's podium—and *still* misspelled half of them. To make up for what I lacked in the ability to see numbers and letters correctly, I did what many people do: I relied on humor. This has been no walk in the park either, since my sense of humor is more like a mild case of Tourette's Syndrome. Political correctness has never been my strong suit. Now combine that with an uncontrollably spontaneous knack of making sexist/racist/religious/political jokes at exactly the wrong time.

Yes, I was generally hated or loved by my high school teachers. If you were an arrogant, self-righteous, bigoted prick of a teacher, chances are you threw me out of your class more than once. I still have no idea what is going to come out of my mouth. Almost everyone who works for me has told me at some point to STFU.

Why do I get away with this? Well, being the size of a small Hummer helps. Take a look at my marquee and you'll know how I *really* feel about issues; look at the movies I book: HOTEL RWANDA, BROKEBACK MOUNTAIN, GUNNER PALACE, ENRON, THE CONTROL ROOM, WHY WE FIGHT, THE REAL DIRT ON FARMER JOHN, GOOD NIGHT AND GOOD LUCK, HUSTLE AND FLOW and so on. You wanna call me on my spotty political correctness, you go ahead and roll that way. Every time I'm up on the marquee trying to remember which way a Q goes, I'm doing what I can for what I believe in. Running a theater in this town is not making anyone rich. But sometimes I can say my piece through the courage of enlightened filmmakers. That gives me the kind of wealth that means something to me, whichever way I spell it.

Something I realized while sorting through all these essays is how really angry I was, trying to make two theaters support themselves in an over-screened town widely known as a great place to raise kids (meaning, stay home and rent videos). This essay was a cute way to vent a bit without coming off as a total ass. The degree of success is in the eye of the beholder.

Frogs

Wouldn't it be nice if we could book movies in advance and have a calendar? In my dreams… So why isn't this happening? Well, the answer is kind of a moving target. Glad I could clear that up for you. You're welcome.

This is my fantasy, you know. To be able to release a calendar of movies that will play when we want them. I get a veritable butt-load of emails from people asking if I'm going to play a movie in current release so they can wait to see it in "the cool theater." This is, like, way-cool that people want to see it in my venue, and it makes my day. But it's also a little frustrating, since often I cannot answer that question. Here are a few of the reasons why we don't have a calendar.

Frog Sex: We have to play low-grossing films. Yep, we often have to kiss a few frogs before we get our prince of a film that pays the bills. Movie companies will often request that we play their lesser titles, like earning our right to play the big ones. It's the carrot on a string, to keep us chasing after their somewhat elusive bigger titles. Now that Carmike has come in, this town is over-screened. So, I play the small stuff, and then when the big ones come out (FAHRENHEIT 911, BROKEBACK, THANKS FOR SMOKING, etc.), sometimes the studios forget about all the scraps I played and give the multiplex the entrees. Ouch.

Half Frog, Half Prince: Sometimes films do just well enough that we would really piss off the movie companies if we stopped playing them. Sometimes the frog doesn't turn entirely into a prince. But, it's prince-like enough that if we stop playing it we get a power-whine from the movie company: "You were still grossing $4 a weekend with our film. Why did you stop playing it? We're not going to give you any more movies if you pull them while they are still making money. Waaaah! Mommmmmmyyyyyy!"

SS Minnow Frogs: Sometimes there are no prints available when it's finally our turn. Movie companies will book a movie with us, and then a few days before we are supposed to play it, they call and say they don't have a print for us to play, but, golly gee whiz, we have this print of Gilligan's Island reruns if you want that. This is when my booker earns his money. He calls around and finds out if there is anything I can play on this end of the continent. Often when a movie you'd never expect to see at our theaters appears, it's usually because it was the only thing we could get in by that Friday.

Flying Frogs: Sometimes films take off. If you had told me we were going to be playing MARCH OF THE PENGUINS for 21 weeks, I would have hurt myself laughing. When we have people lined up out the door to see a movie, it doesn't make a lot of sense to stop playing it just to comply with a calendar we printed.

Frog Butts: Frogs are usually pretty easy to handle. When they get kissed and become princes, things change. Sometimes I get annoyed at movie companies and refuse to deal with them (and vice versa). What if we had booked a couple of films way in advance just so we could have them on the calendar? And what if the company suddenly decides to change the terms of the film rent? I might have to flash them half the peace sign. Typically, we cannot play anything else of theirs until we have paid the ransom…I mean the film rent… they decided to jack up. So, if they knew we had a title of theirs on a calendar, it would not be unheard of for them to use it as leverage to up the film rent on titles leading up to it. "Oh, we decided we need another $1,000 on that film or we're not giving you this one." Not having a calendar allows me to schedule product only after I'm sure they've pulled their heads from their little amphibian asses.

Lying Frogs: If we do a hard-copy calendar and something changes, I can't tell you we never had it. With a website, I can remove a title and deny it was ever there. If we publish it on paper, you can wave it in my face and make fun of me. Hah!

Frustration is a very real part of being in business anywhere. There are always times when the town seems not to support such efforts. It is very easy to lose perspective. The worse thing that can happen is taking oneself way too seriously. For those who are in business, we need a safe place to let that energy go. For me, that place is on my motorcycle, on the road somewhere.

Is This a Small Town?

There are times when Corvallis seems a little small. When I buzz through old box office reports of movies that I loved, that I felt were important but that did almost nothing in the way of attendance, I have to wonder. MURDERBALL, TALK TO HER, MAD HOT BALLROOM—all great films. All sucked total rhino rump in the box office.

These are the types of movies I'm supposed to be bringing to Corvallis, and they are certainly not paying the bills. I'm delighted for movies like MARCH OF THE PENGUINS and MILLIONS that do pay the bills, but you can see these movies at the multiplexes; now that we have so many screens in this town, the chain theater bookers are going after many of the movies that the studios typically used to send to the Avalon. We depend on movies like MY BIG FAT GREEK WEDDING and ELIZABETHTOWN to support the less-promoted films, like INTIMATE STRANGERS and CACHE. When I communicate with other art houses that do not have to pimp out their auditoriums for movies of mass appeal to support their art, I sometimes think Corvallis might be a little too small.

This has very little to do with motorcycling, but it's where I'm going with it anyway. An old friend and I have been riding together since he had a couple of old Kawasakis and I was flogging a right-shifting Norton Commando. Monty looks like your basic old-style biker: lots of tattoos, long gray beard, bald head, and he's about the size of a western state.

I'm awfully particular about who I ride with—an amateur motorcyclist can kill me faster than a distracted teenager making a left turn into my lane while talking on a cell phone, drinking a skinny double soy latte, putting on makeup in the rearview mirror, all the while fishing out a thong wedgie. Newbie motorcycle riders are like eager puppies: they want to ride beside me like they do on CHiPs; they want to try to buy everything that is branded with their motorcycle's logo on it, whether it's the proper piece of equipment or not; they don't know how to ride in a pack without endangering everyone else—and they certainly won't let that stop them from riding in a pack. Yes, many have called me names for not allowing them to ride with me. If you listen carefully, you can hear the Whaaaaaambulance.

There is a quality to motorcycling that brings things into perspective. You see, if you screw up when you're on a motorcycle, you die. Suddenly, the annoyance with the fact that certain "pet" movies fail to bring in what I consider an appropriate number of people becomes insignificant when, out of nowhere, there is a doe prancing stupidly in front of my three headlights. When the expanding and contracting sine wave harmonic of our V-twin motors thunders in my helmet, it somehow acts as a sonar and I know exactly where Monty is in relation to me, even if I cannot see him. It reminds me that not everything is obvious. I sometimes have no idea why I keep flogging the art films in this town, but there is some harmonic between art films and the people who come to see them that resonates with this creature whose chassis I currently inhabit. So I keep doing it.

Last Sunday was hotter than Triplets Whipped Cream Wrestling Night, in case you were stuck in an igloo somewhere. Monty knows I don't do heat well. He can tell you a story about the time we were crossing Montana and Idaho in 100+ degree weather while I was sporting a gangrenous appendix (I thought it was food poisoning; oops). Sunday, he calls me and tells me we are riding to the coast for lunch since it will be about 70 degrees there while it's 100 here. No major arm-twisting needed.

It comes to pass that after salmon and chips we head south on 101. While leaning nicely into a 40 mph corner, the chorus of our engines tells me Monty is about a bike length behind me. It's about 80 degrees, a gust of sea air moves over a field of flowers, and that scent hangs over the road as we breathe through it. Yes kids, this is as good as it gets. Then I remembered this is the way it feels when I take a chance on a little film and someone on the street stops me and thanks me for bringing it to town.

Sometimes, just sometimes, Corvallis isn't as small as I think.

I am addicted to a few websites. One of my favorites publishes snippets of conversations overheard in major American cities from New York to Seattle. Many of these comments are what I would love to say to many of the people I have to deal with on a daily basis. There are times when I come back to Corvallis after traveling and consider the almost obsequious degree of decency with which we treat each other. It borders on the pathological. I mean, who the hell thanks a meter maid for giving you a ticket? But, I've seen it happen here.

We Might Be Too Nice

I get asked a lot of questions…often when I'm standing in line at a store or at the post office, or I'm in front of a urinal spelling a word, or while getting my teeth cleaned, or while staring wistfully into space at the Jackson Street fountain as I drink a cup of coffee, or while standing in front of a urinal wistfully getting my teeth cleaned.

Any question that starts with, "Dude…" almost always get ignored. "Can you spare…" is low on my list of things to respond to. "Are you an Oregon voter?" is only slightly less annoying. But, as Corvalli-onians, we are way too nice. We generally don't respond with east coast verve to the slightest slight. So when I'm asked if I'm an Oregon voter, I just make up a foreign language and pretend I have no idea what they are saying. Singing operatically works, too.

Yes, we are way too nice here. I was in a store recently. Let's say the name of the store rhymes with "orange." I had stopped in to by a "thing." When I originally needed this "thing" a few months ago, the "thing" was only a buck or two. A few weeks ago it was up to three-something. Last week it was up to $5.00.

So, I did not yell, "WTF?" even though that was what I was feeling. For a change, I asked a question.

I wanted to know what happened to price. The clerk, whose name rhymes with "annoyed" told me the manufacturer had raised the prices and "orange" was the first to get them at the higher prices. Not feeling too hometown, I didn't relent. I asked why no one else had raised the price yet. I was told they would soon.

Being a nice Corvallis person, I didn't tell him it sounded a lot like something that rhymes with "twit." The rest of the customers were looking pretty uncomfortable by the time I left—we don't press issues like that in Corvallis, I guess. So, I went to a place that rhymes with "Halibut for Manatees" and got my "things" for about ten cents on the dollar. Being the curious sort, I went to another Corvallis establishment, and discovered "things" had been freshly restocked at $2. A week later I was in Salem, where, over the long weekend, across the street from my concession supply place they had built a shiny new home improvement center whose name rhymes with "Loan Repo." Curiosity got the better of me and I went in. The very same item there was 97 cents.

That's less than a fifth of what "orange" was asking. Granted, I'm not one for home improvement stores so big one needs a GPS unit to find the restroom—since it's a good bet no one who works there will know where anything is. But, holy ungodly markup, Batman. Given the choice between getting tweaked locally or driving a few miles and paying one fifth, there's little wonder why people want big box stores in this town.

What has this got to do with anything? Well, I want you spending your money at the Darkside and also at the Avalon (once we get 'er reopened). If there is something that you think we can do to add more value to what we offer, let us know. (No, we are not doing topless snack bar workers. Stop asking. I'd have to wear a hairnet on my chest to conform to health code.)

If you feel we are doing something way wrong, let us know. Don't be nice. Okay, you can be a little nice. Like, don't start the question with, "Hey, you blooming idiot. How about some toilet paper that doesn't feel like cellophane?"

Seriously, let us know when something is not to your liking. I will tell you if I'm lying to you about the answer. Just say, "That sounds a lot like something that rhymes with 'twit' to me." Chances are I will agree. And if you press me I might even tell you the truth. No matter how far I wander into the deep end to answer your question, I will note what you said and do what I can to make it better. Since the Darkside opened, we have redone all the projector images and all the sound (and we are still improving the sound! I said, we are still…). We've also improved our HVAC and brought art into our lobby. These are all things you told me you wanted.

See, we do care. I twit you not.

There may come a day when I do nothing but lounge around eating melon pieces and surfing the Net for velvet paintings of llamas. I hope not. There is something about sinking elbow deep into a machine that transcends the nebulous oscillations of the theater business. I sometimes wonder if I'm a split personality. As I delicately drop the starter from a one-ton van, I'll be considering whether the symmetrical camera work of Kubrick is derived from Kurosawa's earlier work. Then I drop a wrench and move into something that takes on the taint of Eddie Murphy's early work.

Yep, I Get Dirty

I get dirty. A lot. It's a gift. My mother could tell you stories of when I was a kid…if you happened to be a gifted medium, or even an Extra Large. Recently I had the exquisite joy of replacing the power steering pump in my old Dodge Caravan.

For those of us who believe that reading the manual about as useful as searching for two-for-one Big Mac coupons in the First Alternative Co-op Thymes newsletter, the manual I got for this vehicle reinforces that belief—with gusto. I spent over an hour trying to remove the freed-up pump from the undercarriage by following directions. If I'd had two brain cells to rub together, I would have stopped after five minutes of trying to pass this camel of a power steering pump through the eye of the needle of the undercarriage and listened for the far-off laughing of the person who wrote the manual.

"Turn the unit 90 degrees CCW and withdraw over the axle shaft." After the slow realization that the ass-clown who wrote this had never had his hands dirty with anything but nacho sauce, I stopped, climbed out from under the vehicle, waved at the neighbors who were wishing I would mow my lawn rather than work on my cars, then figured out how I'd do it—resulting in me having the damn thing out in 30 seconds.

This left plenty of time for me to mow the lawn. So, instead, I changed the oil. My wife, not one for filth, was amazed how dirty I'd gotten. So much so, she ran in the house and got the camera and took a picture.

Operating a theater hands-on involves oil and hands occupying the same space at the same time. There are several different lubricants for the projectors alone. When something goes wrong, and there is an audience waiting to see the movie, there is no time to be dainty. Removing an intermittent usually involves greased-up hands, over the wrists and almost to the elbows. A sound-head transmission enjoys splattering me with oil, head to toe.

Have you ever wondered why all my theater T-shirts are black? That's the color of projector grease. Yes, I'm usually wearing a theater T-shirt—day or night—and I'd love to tell you it was out of some sense of advertising fanaticism, and I would, if you stopped me on the street. But really, it's because I have hundreds of them, and I can work on my car, motorcycle, popcorn machine, or Dodge Caravan and pretend you cannot see the dirt. Frankly, I don't usually notice the grease spots so it's best to wear clothing that allows for the mental slippage.

Recently, I've been giving out (new) T-shirts and stuff before the show on Fridays. Last Friday, I walked in to the snack bar wearing a shirt that had obviously been part of my painting couture. It was suggested by an astute worker I might consider changing it before going in front of an audience. Fortunately, I had a cheesy Hawaiian shirt tucked away in my office. This lack of self-awareness is baffling to some of my workers, since I am terribly obsessive about health code issues. God help you if you are behind the counter working and so much as touch your nose and not wash your hands. I have fired people on the spot for not washing their hands after using the restroom. Some of them have actually been employees.

"You! I didn't hear you wash your hands!"

"I just stepped into the men's room to throw out my coffee cup."

"Don't care! You're fired!"

"But…I don't work for you…"

"Not my problem!"

We had about 20 gallons of paint left over from the Darkside construction. Since I didn't groove on paying the HazMat fees for its disposal, I dumped it on the floor of the Avalon—à la Jackson Pollock. I got really dirty since I was bare-footed. I guess I was quite a sight.

So, if you see me walk into the theater looking like a paper plate on the wall of American Dream Pizza, or like something that lives in a tar pit, do not scream and run in terror. I'm not going to touch the popcorn we serve you. Though I'm not above sniffing my shirts and wearing the one deemed least offensive, I never compromise the quality of the stuff we sell you. Granted, my sense of smell seems to be the first thing to go when I'm in a hurry to get dressed (especially if it's a 60 Minutes crew at the front door), but never my sense of what's clean in the snack bar. One day, I might apply that sense of cleanliness to my yard—though the shock might render my neighbors horizontal.

The parenthetical phrase in this essay about having had two girlfriends at once got me one of the most vile email responses to date. Someone, writing for his wife, suggested that due to the inconsequence of my life, I had to live out these fantasies in my writing. Well, who can argue with that? But if I get only one email taking exception to my "fantasy" of having two girlfriends at the age of 19, then I'd have to agree with both my blond stewardess, rich, supermodel wives that I'm not the one with the problem.

Dangerous Double Girlfriends

O ld stuff is dangerous. How we never got dead is uncomfortably miraculous. The fastest I have ever gone in a car was with my fellow theater guy, Ron. We did one hundred and forty-five miles an hour along the flats leading into a city whose name rhymes with Kanby. Do you think we were wearing seatbelts? Did that overpowered Olds have a single airbag (not counting this writer)? Did it have anti-lock brakes? A parachute? Heck, no. We jumped into the lap of Chance and bounced on Her bad knee while giving Her a noogie. Oh, She has swatted me a time or two. But not nearly as hard as I deserved.

A long time ago, before humans walked upright, I started my projectionist career in the booth at a drive-in. Like we do now at the Darkside, we dealt with a couple miles of 35mm film per feature, but we did it quite differently. To toss an image onto that white monolith of a screen in the great outdoors we needed a lot of light (overcoming ambient light was just the start of our problems).

Xenon bulbs were mighty expensive back then (manufacturing them was harder with all the humans not walking upright), so we used a carbon arc light source (not a bulb). Enclosed in huge, steel lamp houses, each lamp had two 13.6 mm carbon rods kept in close enough proximity that an electric arc would jump between them. A damned bright arc, I might add. This was powered by a generator about the size of a small refrigerator or a Prius. So, stay with me here, we had an arc of, oh, say 75 amps leaping through a half-inch space in a metal box behind a projector. Are you seeing Frankenstein's laboratory?

Since film automation was just a gleam in its daddy's eye, we did what was cleverly called a "changeover." Every eighteen minutes—at the end of each reel—we had to change from one projector to another. So we had *two* of everything: projectors, power supplies, and snapping, sputtering arcs. To this day, you might notice when viewing a movie that every eighteen or so minutes a dot will appear for less than a second in the upper right hand corner. These are not called "cigarette burns" like they were called in FIGHT CLUB. Their inspired tag is "changeover cues." When the attentive projectionist saw the first dot, he/she/it started projector two. Ten seconds later, the second dot told them to shut off the image and sound from projector one and turn on the sound/image on projector two. Most of the time the audience never knew what we were doing because the transition was seamless.

Occasionally when one's girlfriend had us distracted, or we'd be in the "reading room," or deep-frying the perfect Pronto Pup (or all three), we would miss a changeover. Thus our thundering up to the booth while the honking and light-flashing audience watched white light flicker on the screen.

Doesn't sound too dangerous to you? Well, let's see you run up a flight of stairs with your Levis around your ankles (especially if the *other* girlfriend is waiting at the top of those stairs with her arms crossed). Actually, the dangerous part was the arc lamps. We had to change the carbons after every couple of 18-minute reels. So, having the power off was somewhat handy if we didn't want to be reduced to $1.98 in minerals on the floor of the booth. Since water was used to cool these high amperage carbons, getting them changed before they burned through the water jackets was high on our list of things to do. Water + Amperage = Mourning Loved Ones. And them pesky carbons got white hot. And they rolled. Often toward you. Often under a cabinet. Or under a projector base. Where that greasy paper towel ended up. More than once we hoped that the fire extinguisher pressure dial resting on zero was wrong.

Ironically, Ashcraft was the brand name on these carbon arc lamp houses. Ironic, because the carbons produced a lot of ash when burned. Movie guy Ron still has one of the old carbon arc lamps in the booth at the Fox Theater in Dallas. And it still works! A highly skilled technician visited the projection booth recently, to install a new exhaust fan to draw off the heat from the xenon lamp. The tech's inability to read arrows resulted in his installing the fan upside down. So, instead of removing the heat from the lamp, it pushed air back in. Since the old carbon arc lamp was on the same duct as the xenon lamp, it got pressurized, filling the projection booth with decades of ash. This is as bad as letting a puppy pee in your laptop. They've yet to find the technician's body.

Ron still has that Delta 88 we were in when we brushed against mach one. It's keeping company with about 70 other cars. (While I was chasing anything that had a female pulse, he was collecting anything that had a pulsing GM V-8.) When I visit his "car farm," I peek under the green Olds' car cover and pat its hood. Today there are a lot of production cars that will do 145 mph (a few of them hybrid!). But, I get some visceral charge out of using horsepower and rugged iron gears to get speed, rather than suppository-esque aerodynamics and weight-saving composites. Kind of like producing light with electrons leaping through air, rather than within the safety of a xenon, gas-filled glass bulb. Al Gore, forgive me…

Things are changing. Cinema has functioned roughly the same way for 100 years. Enter the Digital Age. What used to be grains of silver embedded in polyester, rattling through sprockets and rollers, has been replaced by streaming 1s and 0s. I was moving at 24 frames per second when I was overcome by an image scanning at 30 scans per second. And it crept up on me like I was standing still.

Digital Age

I had two things happen recently that snapped some of my thoughts on digital cinema into focus. For those not up to speed, movie companies want the world to convert to digital cinema since it will cut back on their print production and distribution costs. They say it will end scratched prints and film breaks forever. Yeah, whatever. These are the same people that think I should pony up $100,000 per screen to install their equipment. That'll happen about the time God announces that the only people getting into heaven are married gay couples who raise guide-chinchillas and sell their guano as a tasty after-school snack.

First thing that happened: I was standing with a filmmaker in auditorium four of the Darkside, looking at a movie he'd shot in 24 frames per second digital. It looked pretty darn good. Then he said. "Do you think that looks as good as 35mm?"

The second thing that happened: I had dinner with someone who has even more of a background in black and white photography than I. It is not too often you find people who loved, I mean really loved Tri-X, and have stories like printing a negative before it had been fully fixed (then tossing it back in the fix. Try that with T-Max), tasting chemicals to make sure they were still good, and doing things to cameras you usually only see in monster truck shows. It reminded me how much information there is in one 35mm Tri-X negative and the things we did to get that info onto a piece of photo paper.

And now, a seemingly irrelevant segue, but stick with me here: My mom had a sense of humor. I hope you were sitting. When I was a kid in the '60s, racism was something very near the surface even in the then-sleepy little coastal town of Santa Cruz. My mom, not being a native Yank, loved the idea that this country was a mixture of *all* peoples. I have a picture of her taken on the day she was naturalized, holding a small American flag and her papers. She was very proud. So, she had little use for racism, yet an amazing ability to pick her battles.

Back in the day, there was a TV show named Room 222. It featured one of the first black characters on TV who was a teacher, and he even taught white kids. The horror. So, when some idiot started going off about MLK, Malcolm X, or any other black man of the day, she would look at them and ask sincerely, "Isn't that the guy from Room 222?" Then she would look at me, daring me not to laugh. A losing proposition for a 10 year-old kid. That usually rendered the ranter speechless with wonder at how this rantee could be so clueless. The joke was on them. Though I never got her to stop using the word "negro," the first time I remembered her hitting me was when I innocently used the "N" word in a rhyme.

So whenever someone opines that digital presentation looks as good as 35mm, I feel like turning and asking them "Isn't that the guy from Room 222?" The short answer is, "No. Digital cinema is nothing like real film."

Here's the rundown: digital has a contrast ratio of 1:4. Film: 1:40. Digital film frame: maybe 6 Megs of info. Film: 18 million bits. If a digital projector blows a board, you're down for the night. A 35mm projector is mechanical and can almost always be fixed with twist ties, WD-40, and the love of Jesus in your heart—thus avoiding losing the show. Film technology has been around for a century. Digital technology, about a minute and a half. When I look at the digital pictures I shot on my last motorcycle ride, they look pretty cool. But they suck total goat cheese compared to what you can do with a Tri-X negative. The digital is a compromise. I had to lose detail in the highlights and shadows to get the effect I wanted. Those details would have been there in a 35mm B&W print.

Cinema is about suspending disbelief. The more information on the screen, the easier it is to move yourself into the filmmakers world. Now, the inquiring filmmaker did in fact make a film so good that it could've been shot on VHS and it still would've worked. But bad film really, really sucks on digital. Lots of stuff is getting made these days because it is cheaper to do digital and anyone can get their hands on the equipment. The da Vinci Days film festival screeners wade through hours of less interesting fare before putting out the small percentage of awesome entertainment for you to see. When you watch a 70mm print of LAWRENCE OF ARABIA, you will see how far away from film digital really is. Yes, someday digital will be the same or better than what David Lean could do with Peter O'Toole and Panavision. Today ain't that day. Tomorrow ain't looking too good, either.

Dealing with the public can be trying. But dealing with the public at night can be something completely different. When I was going to college, I worked the graveyard shift in a convenience store in a rather seedy part of a big town. The stories I have from that time are not suitable for such a refined group as those who subscribe to my email newsletter. Let's just say, I developed a sense as to who is trying to scam me and who might not actually be out looking for anything they can get.

The Homeless Guy

Someone recently asked me what was the strangest thing I've had happen at the Avalon. I started a story about an intelligent gas from Pluto appearing in the lobby before the show, gossiping about the relative merits of air fresheners with flatulent Swedish triplets…

Occasionally, it strikes me I'm not nearly as funny as I think I am. Usually I'm broadsided by this revelation when the person I'm speaking to has an expression that can best be summed up by the initials: WTF. At this point I usually pretend like my cell phone is ringing, I answer it with, "Hi, Mom…No, I'm not at home. It's a cell phone, Mom…It goes with me. I don't have to be at home to answer it…" I look up at my victim, "This may take a minute." They usually wander away.

The strangest thing to happen at the Avalon (that didn't involve Jell-O wrestling) started on a dark and stormy night. The type of night no self-respecting intelligent gas would be caught dissipating in. A few brave souls wandered in from the streets to watch a movie. It was that time in the Oregon winter when cabin fever overcomes bad weather, with the need to go from one warm building to another. One lone man carefully stomped his feet dry and waited his turn at the back of the line. When he got up to the counter, it was pretty obvious this was not someone who had a place of his own to go after the show. He dug out pockets of change and set them on the counter for counting. He was short by a couple of bucks, but I pretended he wasn't and he watched the film.

He was the last to leave. With a degree of timidity usually reserved for bothering sleeping Rottweilers and other politicians, he asked if he could wait a spell before going out. I did my paperwork while he sat on the sofa and commented about the movie—thus removing the suspicion he had slept through the whole thing. Au contraire. He grasped the whole thing quite well and spoke of it intelligently. He was watching the clock and seemed to be counting when looking at it. Then as if an alarm had gone off, he leapt up, thanked me 85 times for the movie and being allowed to hang out, and disappeared into the rain.

After that, he came in a couple times a month wearing the same dark overcoat, ball cap, grey hair, and scruffy beard, looking the part of a pirate or Nick Nolte's drinking double. He would start with the change exchange when he got to the counter, I would snag a few quarters, then let him in. One night after the show he asked me why I didn't take all his change for the movie. I told him that it takes too long to count and I gotta keep the line moving. From then on, it was ones. No more coins. I would tell him he gave me one too many bills, and return one or two. Often I gave him a soda or popcorn with the big-toe-in-the-sand routine, "Someone ordered it and didn't want it. Can't sell it. Shame to throw it out…" He'd try to pay me. Once he insisted and handed me a five. He tried to run off. I told him to wait for his change. I gave him five ones. Don't think he noticed.

He never smelled of alcohol or was excessively dirty. He was deferential to the other customers and made his requests with the smallest voice he had. He had his favorite seat, but he could make do if someone got to it before him, though he would look like he had just watched a puppy being put to sleep. He always came alone and was the last to leave. If I didn't appear busy or have company, he would stay to comment about the movie. He genuinely loved film. Whatever road led him to where he was, it wasn't the cinema that sent him into the ditch.

Then, on another dark and stormy night, he came in late for the film, which was not his way. I tried to wave him in but he stopped at the counter. He wanted to pay. I told him he missed part of the movie so I wasn't going to charge him. He stared at me. Usually he avoided anything that even flickered toward eye contact. Okay, this was different. He very pointedly stated that I needed to tell him how much he owed me for all the times I let him in for nothing or close to nothing. I said he owed me not a thing and that he was missing the film. He reached into his pocket and glared at me. Well hell, this could go badly, thinks me. Then he pulled out a wad of money and slammed it onto the glass top of the candy case. Bills, of all denominations. He told me to take what he owed me. This was the first time I noticed this guy was about my size and probably a lot more used to pain than I was. Tentatively, I reached into the pile on the counter and fished out two tens and a five under his steely glare. His tone dared me to lie when he asked if that was enough. I nodded. To say he crammed the money back in his pocket would be an understatement, but we'll stick with crammed. He went into the auditorium. When I turned up the house lights at the end of the film and came back downstairs, he was not in the lobby. He was not in the auditorium. He was gone.

That was the last time I saw him.

I have no idea where he got the cash. It did strike me that he might be illiterate. It became clear the thing with the change was a way to get me to count out the money for him, and he seemed confused. He wasn't lazy. He just couldn't tell the bills apart, or one coin from another. So he had a strategy to get by. God knows I have my share of strategies to get by.

There was nothing remarkable about him for a long time. He was just a collection of idiosyncratic ticks and words that kept him at a distance and me and my customers at ease. He became remarkable when he started acting the way he looked. It was like he held out as long as he could. But, once the cat was outta the bag and I saw the anger that might have been his undoing, he didn't come back. This is a reminder of how thin this shell of civility that delicately surrounds us really is. For most of us, cracks are easily repairable: we get pissed, we get over it. For this guy, the shell broke, and all the king's horses and all the king's men couldn't put him back together again. So, he silently dodged out the back door into the thundering rain.

Necessity is a Mutha. The original plan for the Darkside was a couple of 100-seat auditoriums. Such a plan violated some regulation or other, designed to separate the men from the boys in the building game in Corvallis. So, I was stuck with rooms of less than 50 seats each. Well, sometimes you have to go with what you can do rather than what you wanna do. When problems come up with small auditoriums and too many people, it's time to get creative.

Rube

Pulitzer Prize-winning cartoonist Rube Goldberg (1883-1970) was famous for drawing comically complicated and contrived devices designed to do simple things. For example, he might attach a flying kite to a valve on a helium bottle, which would inflate a phallic-shaped balloon that would fly over a church as the preacher was leaving, so that he would step back in horror onto a rake that would flip up, which would pull a string that went to a lever that opened a gate, so that a ball would start running down a spiral trough, which would lead to a switch that would turn on a hot plate that would boil water in a tea pot, so that when the water boiled it would spin a gear that would raise a rainbow flag that would cause Ann Coulter to scream like a little girl, so that a wine glass on a balance would break and tilt, lowering a fuse into a candle flame... You get the picture.

Rube Goldberg can eat my shorts.

When presented with the possibility of playing AN INCONVENIENT TRUTH, I was asked if I had a way to play the movie to more than just 50

people at a time. No problem, I lied. I can show it to a 100 people at a time…
sure I can. So I found myself sitting in the air-conditioned booth of the
Darkside, looking at two 35mm projectors that had to play the same single print
of a film at the same time. Now, no two projectors run at *exactly* the same speed.
One will always be taking up more film than it is being fed. This means the film
will be stretched between the two projectors and could snap, or it will be piling
up on the floor between the projectors, depending. Since neither of these
options is cool, I had some thinking to do.

If I ever get my own show on the Discovery Channel, it will be called
Twisted Redneck Engineering. I rigged up a kind of yo-yo device between the
projectors that allowed a certain amount of slack/take-up between the
projectors.

However, since the movie is about one and half miles of film long (not an
exaggeration), a variance of even 1% in projector speeds would result in 80 feet
of film on the floor. Highly uncool. So, I had to figure out a way to regulate the
speed. After running a few junk previews that I could afford to risk breaking
between the two projectors, I determined which projector ran faster. Okay, not
too tough to rig up a switch to turn off the speedy projector, slowing it down
when it starts yanking the film too tightly.

Let's hear it for Robnett's Hardware and Searing Supply, and all the cool
stuff they have for people like me.

Next, we threaded up a film and let 'er rip. When tension gets too tight, the
switch cuts power to the faster projector and keeps the film from breaking.
Worked like a charm…until I checked the auditorium. The dialogue sounded
like someone was getting hit intermittently with a cattle prod or injected with
Quaaludes. A little unsettling. So how do we slow this sucker down without
having the actors sounding like they're speaking their lines while getting a
massage? Well, they make this thing called a Variac that's like a giant dimmer
switch for electric motors. Problem A: I ain't got one. Problem 2: They don't
give 'em away. So, I needed to come up with a way to reduce the motor's speed
without using a device specifically designed for that. Time to adjourn to the
"thinking couch" to examine the insides of my eyelids for clues.

Then a light bulb went on. Literarily.

I put a light bulb between the faster projector's power and its motor. The
resistance slowed down the motor. And it cost less than anything in a cup from
a coffee shop. But I needed more resistance, so I added more bulbs.

We kept adding bulbs…and more bulbs, of varying wattages. It takes the
faster projector about half an hour for the speed to stabilize, but by screwing in

and unscrewing bulbs of different sizes during that first half hour, we can adjust the resistance in the power feed to sync up the projectors. You will not see it on the screen because the speed variances are so small it's unnoticeable.

The damned thing worked! All weekend it ran and the only time the movie stopped was when a bad splice from the previous projectionist broke. Even then, Gerry and I had the movie back on the two screens in less than five minutes. We so rule.

Rebekah of snack bar fame said that our OSHA-approved projector interlock looked like something that makes toast in a WALLACE AND GROMMET movie. Jeff found the bulbs "strangely intriguing." He was staring at them like he was watching his dryer at the Laundromat. I think Flynn hit it right on the head when he said, "Somewhere a hamster in an exercise wheel is turning Rube Goldberg over in his grave."

I take a bit of a chance when I write in depth about the technical side of what happens in the projection booth. A lot of people feel it brings them closer to the movie—allows them to appreciate the complexity of the process. Others do not want to see the wizard behind the curtain. Most find it interesting, judging by the emails I receive. Those who don't, seem to be able to forgive me and move back into the disconnection from the technology that perpetuates the suspension of disbelief.

More Digital Drama

I have more time to write these days. Some might see this as a good thing. Others have about had it with my pontificating. Either way, the Darkside is getting her legs underneath her and I've been able to slowly wean her from my teat of constant attention. Apologies for that image.

So, that means I get to think about stuff, like who knows how much longer movie film will be part of your cinema experience. So much energy is being put into digitizing our lives, miles of celluloid film will soon be replaced by a gaggle of electrons bouncing around a silicon chip. It is as inevitable as me being long-winded. And as much as I'd like to rattle a wooden sword in the leather scabbard of Luddite-ism, I will *not* give up my cell phone, PowerBook, or iPod. But there's something about film.

I love that shiny, bendable medium that I can run between my fingers on its way to the projector. For decades I have watched small frames of still images sequenced on a magic ribbon wander away from me at a foot and a half a second, to be devoured by a 60 year-old collection of gears and sprockets passing light powerful enough to melt any frame that spends more than 1/60th of a second in its gaze. Then each of those one-square-inch frames is rendered onto the screen at 20,000 times its original size! Not just once, but 24 times per second. And the technology that does this has hardly changed for almost 100 years. That, to me, is utterly amazing. And that technology will be going the way of Phrenology within the next few years.

So, I want to write about it. I want to say that this film stuff existed. I want to go on the record having said that cinematic experience all started with a square of film in front of a candle. Soon the magic behind the curtain will no longer be that magical. It will be a very precise array of electronics easily controlled by anyone with the IQ of a fern and a decent remote. No longer will there be shutters to be timed and intermittents to be topped off with Lubraplate, and gates to be cleaned and platters to be adjusted. Soon a projection problem will be solved by swapping out a board—a job that can be done by the kid who was flipping burgers just the week before, with all the warmth and affection that same kid has for a piece of chewed gum. (Unless it is a very special piece of chewed gum. You know, one shaped like Richard Nixon's head or something.)

The machinery that moves the film to and from the projector is called a platter system. If a platter motor dies, the film will not be transported to and from the projector. Often a projectionist can feed the film by hand if this happens. Almost every projectionist who works for me has spooled off a whole movie spinning the platter, one hand over the other. One dark and stormy night in the Avalon, Stacey spun the film feed platter by hand while I disassembled and rebuilt its motor. I was sandwiched between two moving platter decks for almost an hour working in almost no space while Stacey held the flashlight and manually kept the platter in sync with the projector. No one in the auditorium knew we were inches away from canceling the show, but we worked together and pulled it off. One time a platter system dumped 2000 feet of film onto the projection booth floor. We managed to get it back onto the platter without stopping the show.

Were you there when the projection bulb blew at the Darkside, and Flynn went into the auditorium to give an interpretive reading of the poetry of Leonard Nimoy? Those ten long minutes before the lamp house was cool enough to get my hands in there went much quicker hearing laughter coming from the auditorium. Did you see the pictures of the system I built to run one movie through two projectors? These days will be gone, like tears in the rain. So today I write about them.

When push-button projection replaces hands-on projection, will anyone care? After all, it's the product that matters. How it gets to the screen is not terribly relevant. I suppose. But if I hadn't fallen in love with the machinery of movies (as well as cinema itself), I could have just worked in a video store instead of building an art house theater in Corvallis, Oregon. It is not rocket science to build a theater and toss flickering light on a white sheet hung on the wall. But the love is expressed when you take responsibility for the 100 people watching the film and make double-damn sure the show goes on with the best presentation possible. And that means everything from dealing with the stomach flu while running the projectors between trips to the restroom, to walking into each auditorium to check the sound system, and looking for that piece of dust dangling into the frame. I had to learn to ignore the people who complain no matter how well the show goes. Instead I take nourishment from those who can see in my eyes how pit-of-my-stomach tired I am and take a moment to say, hey.

If you think running a movie is easy, then we have done our job. It will be easy when it's all done for us digitally. But today, to get two hours of flawless presentation can often mean hundreds of hours of hard work and training. Today, as with all the decades leading up to today, the difference between the show going on or not is the ability of the projectionist to hear a slight change in the pitch of the platter motor and to say, "Well, that ain't right." And then to go look. To rush his or her happy ass into the booth and evaluate the film, the projector, and the image—and know what to do to fend off a film break.

This is what I want to write about. Someday people will look at a film splicer the way my kids look at a rotary phone, and the way their kids will look at my first cell phone. I want for there to be something written that says, "It was hard, hot, often dangerous work to get that movie on the screen. Thank God I got a chance to do it before movies became nothing but bits of data on a flash memory card." Just as Phrenology led to modern psychology, moving pictures in a flipbook led to the immersive experience of the cinema. I know a few shrinks who would argue Phrenology will cure more people than what much of head-shrinking offers today. I hope to seem that silly one day, arguing the virtues of film "against an anonymous wall of digital sound" as Neil Young so aptly put it.

Will I ever forget how to thread a projector? No. It is now a physical memory that lives in my fingers like middle C lives in the fingers of a pianist. Any musician can play a CD, just as any projectionist can play a DVD. That doesn't make it the same thing as creating the music or keeping the show on the screen.

In 1988, when I became the manager of the old movie house in Lebanon, the previous owners regaled me with stories of strange occurrences. Most of it got a generous lift of the eyebrow from me, and little else. By the time I left in 1997, I had names for three different apparitions and they all had different personalities. There are a lot of places I've been that have that "feel" about them—something from "around the bend" is hanging out. Just like any minority, be they solid or not, with enough exposure, their presence just becomes part of the human landscape.

The Kuhn Theater is Haunted!

T he Kuhn Theater is haunted. That will not surprise many people in Lebanon, Oregon, where this theater occupies a place on Main Street, like a book of ghost stories on a shelf of less interesting literature. I ran that theater for nine years, so I know. Cue heavy pipe organ music: Toccata and Fugue in D minor.

The Kuhn Theater was built shortly after the Pilgrims landed on Plymouth Rock in their Dodge Mayflower—the one with the push-button gear shifter that came only in Puritan White. That was about 1930. A single screen affair, the Kuhn was noted for being, um, a movie theater, I guess. About 300 seats and an art deco décor slowly trashed over the decades. Things that were cool about the Kuhn: the mezzanine. It overlooked the main lobby where the giant glass ball chandelier hung. And really cool staircases.

When I started running the Kuhn in the later 1980s, the previous manager told me there were strange things that sometimes happened in the theater when the show was over and all the people had wandered off. He told tales of lights being turned off and on, and stacks of coins being mysteriously knocked over. Cue heavy pipe organ music.

I had been there a couple of years before this irascible, intangible twit of an apparition decided to play with me. Oh, you laugh. But, I was the one in the projection booth breaking down a film for shipping one dark and stormy night.

I was alone in the building, so I thought it odd to hear footsteps. I stepped out of the booth. Nothing. I looked down the stairs to the lobby. No one was there. I shrugged and went back to the booth and got back to work.

A few minutes later I hear a chuckle. Not a malicious chuckle, like Satan or the guy who told you they'd have your car done by the end of the day. More like a "Well, that's kinda funny" chuckle.

I stepped out of the booth. I heard footsteps again, around the corner to the mezzanine. I followed the sound around the corner, and then I heard footsteps on the other stairway. As I headed over there, I heard the chuckle again. My sense of humor was waning the longer I was dragged all over the building chasing an elusive guffaw.

I stomped down the stairs to the lobby. The chuckle came again, this time from the mezzanine above me. I started up the stairs and then I stopped dead. Cue much heavier pipe organ music. I was overcome by the feeling that I was not alone. This was not fun. I grabbed my coat and went home to sleep off whatever flashback I was experiencing. The next morning everything felt as normal as ever.

Normal, for the Kuhn Theater, that is.

It was a particularly busy night at the Kuhn. We had just funneled out the first show and were enjoying the eye of calm before the next storm of people arrived for the next show.

I first noticed him out of the corner of my eye. This older man, say, just this side of 140 years, walked past the box office and into the snack bar. The snack bar workers asked him if they could help him. They were ignored as the old guy passed them on his way into the auditorium. Everyone was looking at me. They wanted me to go into the auditorium and find out what was up with the old guy.

I went in, expecting to find him clinging from the ceiling making bat noises. Instead he was sitting in a seat, quietly. I asked him if he thought he might like to buy a ticket. He didn't look at me and just uttered, nearly inaudibly, "My wife died in this very seat a long time ago." There's that heavy pipe organ music again. I went out to the snack bar and told the workers to just carry on and everything was fine. Local legend has it that she's the one adding color to the old building.

My oldest stepdaughter will not go into the Kuhn. After what happened to her, who can blame her?

My stepkids were pretty much raised in the Kuhn. They would sleep at my feet in the expansive box office while I sold tickets, or play up and down the staircases for hours. So, to have one of my kids in there with me late at night was more the norm than not.

This particular night, as we were wrapping up the evening behind the snack bar, a noise came from the closet under the stairs. We both walked over to the closet and slowly opened the door. Nothing. As soon as we started walking away, the noise started again. We looked at each other and snuck back to the closet. I opened the door. Nothing. I shooed the kid back to the snack bar without me. As she walked away the noise started again. I grabbed the knob and slowly turned. My kid smiled like the guy who just told me my car would be ready at the end of the day.

Okay, cue the heavy pipe organ music, already.

I whipped the door open. Inside the closet the broom, dustpan, mop, and other implements were swirling around in mid-air, as if in a tornado. Then suddenly they froze in place, and dropped to the floor. You know that phrase about your blood turning to ice in your veins? In this situation, my blood turned to liquid nitrogen. My kid screamed like the ten year-old girl she was, and ran like hell for the door. The thought of her running into the street after midnight thawed my blood, and I ran after her.

Pull the plug on the pipe organ since that was the last event of this nature. Not a peep from the little fiend for my last couple of years there.

It has been suggested that I have a "gift" for hyperbole; however, I would swear on a thousand billion Gideons that this is the way I remember this story. The old Kuhn is open again, now. It's gone through more than a few ups and downs since I left her in the mid-1990s to build the Avalon Cinema. There is a spirit in the old building. Whether it is some pesky poltergeist or the inability of a community to watch their old movie house go, it's good to see an old theater not being left by the Whiteside. I mean wayside. Did I say Whiteside?

It's a part of the real world: People get jobs and have power over you. A lot of time these people are not the brightest crayon in the box. There are bullies who lord their movies in front of me due to some imagined or long-ago slight—refusing to take my calls or answer my emails. Then there are those who, like me, are just trying to get through their day.

Yes, Virginia. There Are Stupid People.

I don't trust stupid people. Good thing I run a business that caters to smart people. Trust is a huge part of my day. In this little hamlet of ours we generally trust each other to stop at red lights, wait for pedestrians, not ram the meter maids, and so on. I can leave my car unlocked in front of the theater and generally nothing is missing, when I remember not to leave the laptop on the front seat with a neon "Steal Me" sign, and the stacks of hundred dollar bills are cleverly disguised with one-dollar bill wrappers. Foolish car breaking and entering persons...

When I was young and foolish, I found myself in a boxing ring, wearing silly, red, oversized gloves. My training guy started me with, "I ain't trainin' you to kick anyone's butt. Yer gonna just tap this guy to get points. Swing in, tap him, get out before he lands one on ya."

I was a skinny preteen who thought it would be pretty cool to be able to beat a guy in a fight without having to beat him or fight him. Kinda like touch football. This day, the kid I was up against was the size of a mule and about as smart. He was the type of guy who could have an onomatopoeia splat him right in the face with a mighty bop, and he'd have no idea what went kerpow.

With the ring of the bell he stepped into the ring and swept with one huge gloved hand, hoping I just happened to be in front of it. I easily dodged his lumbering swings, and for each of them I landed three or four point-counting "punches." He was becoming more frustrated and stupider. The stupider he got, the easier it was to stay out of his way. I didn't mean to taunt him. I was all business. He lunged at me. I stepped aside and nailed him a couple—hard enough to ring up points but not exhaust myself.

The fifth round of dodging and poking had just ended and the bell rang. I dropped my guard and turned my back and started toward my corner. This kid lunged at my back and landed a punch squarely on one of my kidneys. It was the only time in my life I felt my legs just say "Adios, amigos" and fold up. Down I went, smack onto the matt. Then the pain set in. I rolled over in time to see this huge kid looming over me, laughing. Suddenly the coach grabbed him by his shoulder and dragged him into his corner. Another adult was helping me up and slowly my legs were getting the message they had a job to do. But, my legs weren't hurting. My back felt like I'd been hit by a low-flying plane. When I turned and looked at the kid who'd floored me, he was in his corner, now crying. My coach was yelling at him—something about me holding back and the next fight will be with no gloves and he was gonna let me wipe up the floor with him. At that moment, I didn't feel capable of wiping my own nose.

The lesson I learned was to never turn your back on someone with limited intelligence, especially when they are frustrated. Not that I'm the sharpest knife in the drawer, but when I'm up against a wall, flailing stupidly has never served me.

I have an unusual amount of trust for my customers. You are smart people. Most of you are much smarter than I am. This trust goes a lot deeper than the money that gets passed through the mail slot at the Avalon when you forgot your wallet and I tell you to pay me later. You have been the guiding force behind many of the decisions I make about the theaters. Like I said, you're smart.

I book my movies by what you tell me. Okay, not exclusively. I do research on the Net and listen to my booker tell me how a certain movie has fared in similar markets. But, you are the ones who give me my best ideas. You hounded me for months before MARCH OF THE PENGUINS was even a faint blip on my booking radar. You hassled me en masse about AN INCONVENIENT

TRUTH long before I knew it was a 90-minute Gore-a-thon about global warming. Like I said, you're pretty smart.

I never went back in the ring after that big kid knocked me down. I wasn't so much scared of getting knocked down, as I was of having to share a ring with a stupid person who would turn a boxing match into a fight. I've never been that athletic, but the few things I could do well didn't need to be contaminated by some clown getting mad and changing the rules.

I see this the same way I look at the type of movies we play. There are rules to this game. I try not to play crap. Oh, there are lots of films where people leave and ask what I was smoking when I booked that movie. Lots of my films piss a lot of people off. But that's part of my rules: nothing too safe.

If I wanted safe, I could book by looking at the national box office grosses. That would eliminate directors like Pedro Almodovar (TALK TO HER, ALL ABOUT MY MOTHER), who will always be played in my theater. It will be a cold day in hell before I will consider anything from Steven Spielberg (WAR OF THE WORLDS, MINORITY REPORT).

As long as you show up, and buy tickets and popcorn to see art films, I will play them. If you stop showing up, I'll try to resist the urge to go to mainstream crap. I'll throw in the towel and choose my next fight very carefully. I've lived through having my legs knocked out from under me—many times. That isn't too scary. Waking up and asking myself what I've become scares me.

Most of us have friends from our childhood we don't think about until something brings our minds back to those years when there was nothing more important than the games we played in the neighborhood. As we move into adulthood, as it were, playing seems to take a seat further and further in the back of the bus. Sometimes the memories of simpler days collide with the complications of the last half of our lives.

Anthony

When I was a wee lad of nine years old, I asked my mom how movies were made. Since I had just torn her sewing machine apart to see how it worked, she answered with a certain trepidation. But the next day she handed me the Bell & Howell 8mm movie camera and a roll of film. Threatening me with slow death if I took the camera apart, she showed me how to load it and gave me the two-minute lesson in animation. So, with my GI Joe and my teddy bear, I made my first stop action movie. Thus was spawned the addiction that monkeys my back to this day: movies.

My partner in these cinematic crimes was my good friend and neighbor, Anthony. He was a stout, enthusiastic kid, and part of the Catholic gaggle next door. Like me, he enjoyed going on money hunts to vending machines and phone booths (to support our movie film/processing habit), collecting aluminum cans on the Santa Cruz beaches, spying on the nude sun bathers, building coasting carts to race down the hill behind our houses, and—bonus!— his dad owned a bicycle shop. Anthony was also terribly dyslexic. It seemed to him that school's only purpose was to make him feel stupid. But his brilliance was in his creativity, and his ability to tear anything apart and rebuild it before he got busted—that last part an ability my mom wished I had.

Anthony was my special effects man: he figured out if you put a catsup pack and a firecracker under a GI Joe's shirt, it looked like he'd been shot—that is, if you could ignore the hand coming into the frame to light the fuse. When we strapped the movie camera to the front of the coasting cart, he would start from the very top of the hill—an act I suspected was sure death—so we could get more speed. With the camera mounted with masking tape and hope to the front of this coasting contraption, he defied death at what was surely 15 mph. I was sure we'd got an awesome shot until it struck me we hadn't considered the stopping part of this run. Evidently, it had slipped Anthony's mind, too, right up to when he ran out of road. I watched him tear the camera from its mount and smoothly slip off the cart, which shortly after was greeted sternly by the curb. He rolled to a stop holding the camera aloft. It was unhurt. He had looked better. Then we discovered we'd forgotten to lock the shutter release into the "On" position. Anthony was ready to do it again, right then. I called it a day. I was the director. I could do that.

Our neighborhood was rife with WWII veterans, so we had all the accoutrements of soldier-dom a couple of preteens with a movie camera could want. We staged battles with real army uniforms and real army canteens and real army holsters (holding our real western cap guns) and real army helmet liners (the metal ones were too heavy for us to wear) and real army ammo belts and boots. Everyone in the neighborhood had something to offer us when they saw the camera come out.

Once we stuffed Anthony's brother's wetsuit with newspaper and put a uniform on it, and had my brother toss it from a cliff for a dramatic end to a scene. It fluttered to the ground with all the limbs articulating like a string of sausage links rather than a human body, but we thought it was perfect. My mom became my cameraperson, and every kid in the area wanted to be in the movies we shot. We would try to finish shooting early enough to get the film to Longs Drugs for processing before they closed. After the week slogged by waiting for the film came back, we would all collect in the dark of my hallway to watch the masterpiece. The flickering light reflected back from the white door we used as a screen, playing across the faces of way too many kids crammed around an old cranky projector. We witnessed how Anthony— with annoying predictability— would wave at the camera at least once each roll. So much for staying in character and not looking at the camera.

As I climbed into my teen years, my time in Santa Cruz came to an end and our family traded the warm sun of California for the frigid rains of British Columbia. As the Viet Nam war wore on, my appreciation for all things military was left behind like my worn out cap guns. I became more interested in stop-action animation and then segued into still photography. Anthony fell into the background of my memory, as I was now a thousand miles away from Santa Cruz and he wasn't much for writing. And the decades rolled by.

It had been 35 years since I had seen Anthony, though I thought of him often. A couple weeks ago I stopped by his family's bicycle shop in San Jose and found his brother, Alex. He didn't recognize the 13-year-old he used to live next door to, but I clearly remembered the 16-year-old who used to torment me. It was a good reunion, but he wouldn't say too much about Anthony except that he wasn't at the shop and hadn't been—for about a year. One of the other guys told me that a year or so ago, someone had introduced Anthony to crank. Alex said he had to have Anthony thrown off the property because he was so out of control with the drugs. I asked where Anthony had landed. On the beaches of Santa Cruz, Alex said. The next day I rode Hwy17 over to Santa Cruz. I found myself cruising up and down the beaches hoping to see someone whom I probably wouldn't even recognize. This ain't my first day at the rodeo, so I knew enough to not let anyone using crank get too close, but I wanted to just see him. Perhaps preserving precious memories, I didn't find him.

With a broken heart, I pointed the Harley down Highway 1 away from Santa Cruz. Nothing that happens these days can permanently take away the joy Anthony and I shared as kids, but it can make it hard to come back to where the love of cinema has led me. As I re-enter my life as a Corvallis movie guy I feel the tug of Santa Cruz, accented by random memories, like the way Anthony used to laugh when I got pissed because he waved at the camera. It's all good. Anthony's soul may have been given over to the evil crank demon, but the kid he was still lives—in the joy I feel when I hear my projectors sing, and see the smiles on the faces of the people who come to my theater.

When people ask me what I do for my day job, I know I'm doing my job well. I'm making it look easy. The fact is, it takes up to 60 hours a week to keep things going at the theaters. The beauty of selling on eBay is that the time is so flexible. So, if one can shoehorn in a couple of hours to cruise thrift shops and garage sales, sometimes a few minutes of work can result in hundreds of dollars.

eBay

I f you needed a "Time To Put An Atheist In The White House" T-shirt to wear the next time your neighbor is wearing his "God Talks To Bush" T-shirt while mowing his lawn, where would you look? If you wanted a Truth Fish eating the Darwin Fish emblem for your car, to annoy your neighbor even further, where would you look?

Started in Pierre Omidyar's living room in San Jose, California, in 1995, so his girlfriend could swap Pez dispensers, eBay has grown into the world's foremost online auction house. Since about 135 million people use eBay and my spell checker even automatically corrects ebay to eBay, it would be safe to say they are onto something.

The other day I was having coffee with Brenda VanDevelder, who is the Grand Fromage of the da Vinci Days Festival. Someone actually asked her what she did the rest of the year when the festival wasn't happening, completely oblivious to the 11.9 months of planning, fund-raising, volunteer coordination, setup, and sleep deprivation each festival requires. She understands the frustration I feel when people ask what I do during the day, since my theaters only run at night. The closest I've come to having an outside job while running the theaters is when the Avalon was first open, and the movie companies seemed to feel they needed to get paid. The "job" that provided the most return with the most flexible work schedule was selling on eBay.

I got my eBay account ten years ago and used it robustly to keep the Avalon afloat at the beginning, until you all started coming around regularly. Now, I have always been addicted to thrift shops, and know them the way Rush Limbaugh knows Oxycontin. Remember, this was almost ten years ago, when the novelty of online auctions was hot enough that people were buying *anything* just for the bragging rights to say they won the bidding. I developed a circuit of thrift store stops that went from Eugene to Portland—a loop I trolled at least once a week.

These were the good ol' days, before the thrift stores figured out that the junk they were almost giving away was being sold online. Now, you can't cross a Goodwill sales floor without listening to someone ask what's up with the pricing—some items priced higher than new. But back in the day, spending twenty bucks could net you hundreds. So you could post anything from used greeting cards to a Betamax video of platypus husbandry and people would be on it like patchouli on a hippie. Some of us who were selling on eBay would make bets on who could spend the least and make the most. I watched a 25-cent brass horse's head picked out of a discount bin go for $25.

Since my fashion sense is about as developed as my operatic singing skills, it was a natural I'd be dealing in Hawaiian shirts. Goodwill would sell them all day for 99 cents, while they sold for up to $80 on eBay. I learned to know the labels that were authentic and the ones sold in tourist shops to overweight tourists in flip-flops who still snickered at the word "lei." If a cool gaudy garment ended up in the thrift shop, there were usually a few obvious reasons: the size label was incorrect, there was a stain or a hole, or it was missing a wooden button you couldn't just pick up at KMart. So I had a garbage bag full of stained and torn shirts labeled: Parts. It got so I could tell across a room if the pocket pattern was lined up with the rest of the shirt and if that hem was actually torn or had just become unstitched. It almost had my biker friends questioning my sexual preference.

As with all good things, thrift shops eventually figured out those shirts were worth something. Soon, the same shirts I started bidding at $9.99 were being sold at that price by Goodwill. It became more of a real hunt to find the deals. I'm thankful I had other areas of knowledge I could exploit, like spotting a Nikon F body in a pile of cheap point-and-shoot cameras, or a tube radio in a cluster of blown speakers. I could divine a 1950s garden gnome from one fresh off the ship from China. So I still did okay. But then the scammers started popping up like weeds in this once fertile flowerbed. They were trying things like threatening negative feedback if you didn't forego shipping charges. Bad checks, shill bidding, items being sent back even though they were sold as-is, people breaking items and claiming the shipper did it was becoming very common. Buyers' remorse—the what-the-hell-was-I-thinking—became an epidemic. Fortunately, the Avalon was starting to get her legs, and I managed to segue out of the increasingly vicious eBay selling world.

But I had some memorable finds. A shortwave radio made in Germany during WWII that didn't work, but turned out to just need a wire in the plug refastened. Paid $25 for it and sold it for $500. An entire shoebox of ViewMaster disks from the 50s and 60s purchased at a garage sale for $5—each of which went for anywhere from $5 to $150. That paid the rent for a while. A box of vacuum tubes that I sold off one at a time for months, at $1 to $25 each. I even sold my worn-out biker boots to someone in Japan for more than I paid for them new. When my feedback rating started to get pretty high, I even found myself getting envelopes from Asia containing American currency, a practice unheard of today.

I still cruise eBay almost daily but I hardly ever sell there anymore. Usually I look for parts for my Harley, my old Mercedes, or my projectors. Mercedes wanted $380 for new hatch struts for my beater wagon. The online parts houses wanted $180. I found them new on eBay for $50. Have you noticed that the image on the Darkside screens is constantly improving? Every time I see a good lens for auction I bid on it.

Selling on eBay always was, and still is, a job. You have to be responsible, and there are always bozos who refuse to be satisfied. That job has gotten harder. Now that eBay has gotten expensive, convoluted, and every second email bearing an eBay header is a scam or sales pitch, it makes me long for the days when I would take a dollar into a thrift store and turn it into $20 by the end of auction. I can say without snickering that without eBay, the Avalon/Darkside Cinemas wouldn't exist.

Sometimes it is the ephemera of our lives that brings us closer to who we are today. Some people in our lives have moved on without us or us without them. But it is the little things that can make them part of our day again. Sometimes it's a scrap of paper with a scribbled note. Often it's a trinket that brings us back to a place well visited. For me, the chronology of the last ten years can be tracked in the posters of the movies we played. This was made clear again as I moved things around to make way for improvements at the Avalon, which we hoped would bring her back to life.

Posters

There is a certain cruelty to flipping through old posters. Rolled up into big colorful, glossy, multi-leafed rolls and stored like bouquets of fresh daffodils in empty popcorn oil buckets, they rest patiently knowing full well the day will come when I unwind them like old papyrus and lay them out flat.

Hidden deeply in the storeroom next to the Avalon auditorium are these posters, which I have been accumulating for nine years. The further I delve into the scrolls, the farther I go back in time. Inevitably, the poster unfolding before me brings back events tied to the showing of its film. The cruelty lies in the realization that I've lost those days when showing art films in Corvallis didn't involve four screens and my absence from behind the counter.

But my day job this past few months—the reclaiming of the Avalon Cinema from the ravages of time, giving her a new face and trying to keep the bills paid—has me drooping by show time. Consider it merciful to not have to see me behind the counter at the Darkside after I've spent the day hauling trash and making nice to the sheetrock gods. Frankly, I reek. And sometimes I'm so cranky that a mouse farting three counties away makes me want to hurt all small, furry animals with explosives. So, it's just as well you've been enjoying Gerry and his affable mellowness, Jeff and his casual coolness, Flynn and his near perfect TV evangelist's smile, and Rebekah and her sly yet motherly humor. The truth is, I miss working shifts. I miss the sass and warmth from you—the people who are part of my community.

Instead, I'm unfurling posters like flags from past campaigns, which is what they are: flags from past advertising campaigns. I loved finding the poster from WINGED MIGRATION and remembering how I started referring to that movie as "crack for senior citizens." We had a lot of gray hair glowing in the auditorium for that movie. Almost as much for AMELIE, which had even the most action-oriented American moviegoer forgetting they were reading subtitles. It got an R rating, but families still showed up and were swept away by her French charms. NINE QUEENS was the magical South American caper film that crowded some of Mamet's best work. A movie that made my work a joy was MOTORCYCLE DIARIES. Boy howdy, was I glad to find another poster for it since the one I squirreled away upstairs fell victim to the leaking roof. That bastard rain did ruin my DONNIE DARKO poster, of which I only had one. One of the longest films we ran was UNDERGROUND—runtime was 3 hours—an amazing Eastern European film about a drunken family living in a basement for generations, thinking WWII was still in full swing in the world above. Its Bosnian director, Emir Kusturica, was the co-star across from Daniel Auteuil in THE WIDOW OF ST. PIERRE, an amazing French film about Gandhi-esque forgiveness. SEXY BEAST, with an unforgiving Ben Kingsley, was the first film we played after I put in the new digital sound system I'd scrimped and saved for. Of course, BEAST was thick with Cockney English accents, so no matter how good the sound system was, you couldn't understand a damn thing they were saying.

And the list goes on: The stunned looks on the faces of people after PI. Widening the gaps between show times for LIFE IS BEAUTIFUL because many were rendered paralyzed from the emotional impact of that movie. People still ask me, "What was that Japanese film about taking your favorite memory into heaven?" That one played eight years ago (AFTER LIFE). The audience's delight during THE DISH, when the Australian band announces the American national anthem and instead whips out a randy rendition of the theme from Hawaii Five-O. I even found two posters from the first-run theater in Lebanon, which I ran before opening the Avalon: CONTACT and AUSTIN POWERS.

And with this history behind her, the Avalon Cinema looks ahead, with newly flattened and decorated floors, reconfigured seating, and a digital presentation. We are going through the process of getting a liquor license to serve beer and wine, but we may reopen before the license or the serving equipment has arrived. We've yet to weather the stormy waters of the requirements to serve pizza, so we will most likely start with the time-honored Avalon Cinema staples: soda pop, popcorn, candy, and bad marital advice. It's time to let laughter ring off her walls again, so we are planning to reopen the doors October 20th! (Is your FlickClique membership up to date??)

I'm sure that ten years from now, I will be unscrolling the poster for the reopening of the Avalon Cinema. A tide of nostalgia will wash over me. However, as the waters of sentimentality recede, the jagged rocks of reality will remind me that it wasn't all sunshine and roses. But, this will be balanced by the knowledge that I will never be one of those who lie on their deathbed asking, "What if?"

And so for now, I send out these self-absorbed pontifications to thousands of people (and God bless both of you who actually read them). It is my way of making contact with you since I'm not working shows. Just be grateful that my absence from the counter keeps the daily accumulation of sawdust in my hair from ending up in your popcorn. Though it actually doesn't taste that bad, I bet you'd prefer brewer's yeast.

I actually like the wind. Guess it comes from so many years on a motorcycle. However, when it gets destructive, my affection wanes. But, there are all manner of ways to pass the time until the power comes back up. Not all of them involve a birth rate increase nine months later.

The Night the Lights Went Out in Corvallis

I t was a dark and stormy night. Literally. That would have been last Thursday night, the night the big storm blew through the western region of Oregon. There's nothing quite like the sound of a swamp cooler ripping loose from its moorings and skipping across the roof, followed by the thud of that 150 pounds of sheet metal and motor greeting the cement wall at the edge of the roof.

Far from amused, I donned my waterproof-est jacket and ascended to the tippy-top of the Avalon Cinema. There be wind! My 230 pounds on the slippery roof was little more than a plaything for the gales coming from the river. I crept over to the swamp cooler and found it literally balancing on the roof edge. Another .5 mph of wind and this three-foot cube of metal would have seriously pissed off the owners of a new Acura and a generic SUV parked directly below. I wrestled the beast back from its suicidal perch, dragged it over to the heater chimney and lashed it tight with a proper pirate's knot. On my way back to the roof hatch, I crested the domed roof just in time to be nailed by the strongest gust of the night. Since just trying to blow me off the roof wasn't enough, it decided to be spiked with debris moving at twice the speed of sound. My face felt like I tried to smoke an exploding cigar. When I got to the roof hatch, I saw its chain had been ripped away by the wind. I slithered down the hole into the relatively eerie quiet of the Avalon upstairs.

Though the power was flickering, it was still on for the handful of brave and hardy people who showed up for the show: KEEPING MUM. At the stroke of 7:00, just as I was about to run a credit card, darkness fell like black oil. The emergency lighting was on in the auditorium so we adjourned to the big room. I usually wait about half an hour when there's a power outage, in case it comes right back up. A couple of bicyclists tucked into their takeout burritos, and the rest of us listened to many, many jokes told by two delightful kids, 8 year-old Rachel and 5 year-old Nathan. Since I have always felt there are two types of humor—clean jokes and funny ones—it became readily apparent that my arsenal of kid-appropriate jokes is quite lean. That was okay. These kids filled the humor vacuum nicely.

The storm was raging like a Klansman at diversity training, holding little promise of the power returning. Lainie, being the smarter half of our relationship, suggested I grab the DVD out of the player and run it in my laptop. Nice idea, but the eject button on the player needs some power to open the drawer. For some reason, these pro decks don't have the paperclip hole that King Arthur undoubtedly used to dislodge Excalibur from its stone. However, I'd been loading movies onto our server. In order to do that I need to uncompress the video files from the disc onto my PowerBook before FTPing them onto the projector server. (Legal note: I'm licensed to play this movie. I *never* do this with movies I am not licensed to exhibit. Do not try this at home.). I just happened to have an uncompressed file of the movie on my hard drive.

Showtime!

We gathered around in the Avalon pillow pit and set the laptop on the stage. I set out a bucket of popcorn and some bottled waters, and then we watched the movie on my tiny PowerBook. Yes, it was very, very quiet.

We hadn't had a chance to get dinner, so while the movie was running, Lainie held down the fort and I made my way to China Delight. I've walked this route a thousand times at night, but with the lights out and traffic left to its unregulated devices, it was quite a challenge to go those few blocks. I tormented Jack at China Delight by making him explain to me why he couldn't deep-fry me a shrimp roll on demand. He finally told me I could get the soup, or the heck out. I ordered the soup, but asked him if he could put it in the microwave for a minute since mine wasn't working at the moment. He gave me That Look.

Though my laptop wasn't completely charged when we rolled the opening credits, the battery worked for about an hour and a half. So, just as the vicar (Rowan Atkinson) was intoning God's voice…the screen went black.

The storm was still dancing on the roof, the kids were having a ball running between all the seats (as mine did at that age), and the grown-ups sat about discussing all things Corvallis. Not an entirely unpleasant way to pass a storm. One of the grown-ups said it was like an X-Files episode: the darkened room and silhouettes speaking in hushed tones against the wind noise. The truth is out there, baby. This time it was clear: the truth is at 24 frames per second.

It wasn't long until the power came back up and suddenly we were shocked back into our world of artificial light. I was going to head to the booth and fire up the projector so the audience could watch the rest of the film on the big screen. A unanimous "No!" erupted from the assembled faithful. They wanted to watch the rest of it on the laptop! I killed the auditorium lights, left the candles lit, and watched the vicar finish his speech.

The winds had subsided, to be replaced by the sounds of emergency vehicles moving through the city. Once I got the "crowd" out with their promise to drive and ride carefully in the chaos, I headed to the roof and surveyed the town. I saw areas with and without power scattered across the townscape.

As I clattered to north town in the bio-Benz, I was amazed at the sporadic nature of the outages—whole parts of town were painted black, and then there would be one block with power. I was impressed by the number of trees knocked horizontal, obscenely displaying their root balls.

Though the Darkside had to refund admissions (a laptop battery just won't power up those 1600-watt xenon projection lamps; funny that), at the Avalon, the show went on in no small part due to the ability of the audience to just enjoy the evening and to flow with what technology we had available. I guess I better brush up on kid-appropriate humor for the next power outage. How about: a biker, a rabbi, a hooker, and Bill Gates are on an airplane… No, wait—that won't do.

This piece was written in 2006, and I was honored to be asked to read it at the 2007 Magic Barrel in Corvallis, an annual event that helps raise funds for Linn and Benton County Food Share. There are those who think watching movies begins and ends with the multiplexes and Netflix. Though these people generally do not subscribe to my weekly missives, sometimes my writing is forwarded to the underexposed, and a small glimmer of recognition might emerge out of my using words like, say, drive-in movie theater.

Drive-in Girl

My familiarity with Portland is more than just passing. A couple of times a month, I travel into the city with thousands of others—all of us distracting ourselves from the monotony of gridlock with our devices: cell phones, music players, hand-held digital devices. All these toys help us dissociate ourselves from the dullness of the outside six-lane world.

I've been doing this for more than a decade. For decades before, I drove in just to be in a city. I came to Oregon from Vancouver, B.C., and there are times that my nostalgia for chaos and humanity draws me to Portland. This day, however, the chaos was like sandpaper abrading my last good nerve. I think it was the construction wearing me down, with surging and bucking for miles at a time. I was forced to adapt to the varying spectacle of brake lights in front of me—ranging from nonexistent to retina-searing laser-guided LEDs.

After a morning of braving the unkind urban traffic to pick up my films for the week, stopping by the Motor Vu Drive-In Theater, in rural Dallas, Oregon, provided a welcome contrast to busy Portland. This was one of those afternoons where you could smell the impending winter in the sun-warmed, flame-colored leaves dripping from the trees.

I dropped the movie film at the door of the projection booth and stood for a moment to watch a cloud of blackbirds move and part in the sky, like a confused weather system. Looking at the forest of speaker posts, a memory clawed over the rock wall of time, and made its way into my day. When I was in my late 20s (just a few short years ago), I worked at this very drive-in theater.

One summer night, I had just chased home the last car after the show, and was closing down the snack bar. I unearthed a box of light bulbs from the back of a cupboard—replacement bulbs for the lights in the speaker posts. I'd drunk too much free, bad coffee during my work night, meaning it would be hours until I could sleep. Instead of settling for late night reruns or rereading old Box Office magazines, I headed to the abandoned field with bulbs in hand. I spent the next several hours cleaning, repairing, and replacing the lighting in each post in the drive-in field. Shimmering in the warm summer night, the hundreds of illuminated speaker posts seemed to form a luminous oasis in the dark. The field glimmered like a scale model of a city I could walk through, like a benign Godzilla.

I was jarred back into scale by a set of car headlights coming in from the exit road. Thinking it might be kids looking for a make-out spot (or worse) I remained still in the field of lights. The car stopped at the snack bar and a young woman with flaming hair and a doll-like face got out, trying to peek into the window of the building. I hung back and asked, perhaps a bit too loudly, if I could help her. Not expecting anyone to be out there, she turned quickly and tried to see me in my glowing sea. She called out that she'd lost her purse. I was suspicious, being that it was about 3:00 am and I didn't remember having seen her at the show that evening.

With her hand over her eyes, the young woman tried to see the voice she heard in the lights. It was obvious she was getting creeped out by my seeing her, but her not being able to see me. She was quite small and, well, I'm not. So I figured she might be even more creeped out if I were to close the fifty-foot gap between us.

I was careful not to seem like I was yelling when I said I had been working and hadn't seen her purse. She now used both hands to shade her eyes against the twinkling. No one had turned it in, I reported.

I remained a good distance from her, in no small part because, if she turned out to be a nut-job, I wanted to be able to say I was never near her. I asked if she'd searched her car. She said she'd been in her boyfriend's car. So, he let her drive all the way out here in the middle of the night, alone?

"Yeah, he's an asshole," she said, like I should have known. So, I agreed. She moved her hand from her eyes and it seemed she could now see me and — for the first time—the storybook glow of the illuminated field.

We could hear the distant sparse traffic while she looked at my lighted landscape, like it was a present freshly unwrapped from under the tree. She laid her arms over the car roof and her expression changed—softening and becoming more present. I slowly turned and saw what she saw: the hypnotic beauty of the cascade of twinkling in the perfect summer night. It took almost a minute before the lack of conversation became heavy in the air.

She broke the spell, got in her car, and started it. She rounded the speaker post and pulled up next to me. Some paranoid instinct told me to back away. She smiled, enjoying the possibility that I might be the one a little creeped out this time. With thanks, she asked if I would call her if it turned up. I said I would, somehow not asking for her number.

Her headlight beams teeter-tottered up and down with each exit road pothole, until they disappeared behind the fence. I found myself waving to her—grateful to have shared that night and my lights, even for just a moment, with someone else.

In my monthly rounds, I continue to travel the I-5 corridor, picking up films and supplies from the Big City. And though I enjoy cranking up a good guitar riff to blot out the sound of a jackhammer, the life-sucking lull of frozen traffic can be tempered by the memory of land-locked stars hovering on speaker posts, separated by a summer night from the constellations above.

This was written at a time when the Avalon had yet to meet her fate, and permanently close. There is a sadness in reading something written at a time when there was so much hope, which soon eroded into a pragmatic decision to close her doors. However, before those doors closed we did play some mighty fine stuff. What follows is an example of what we were trying to do there.

Clear Cut

L eaves are starting to cover the sidewalks, the nipply air is punching through my T-shirt, and my thoughts are turning to herding llamas sporting tutus and horn-rimmed glasses down Second Street, while I'm wearing a bra over my eyes and asking everyone I see to "Take me to your leader." I'm sure your thoughts are, as well.

With the changing of the seasons comes the assessment of how well the summer was spent, since the fair-weather activities will soon be washed away by Oregon rain falling like soy creamer into my Mr. Espresso Gourmet House Blend. One of the reasons so many of us are addicted to coffee is that it is brewed sunshine we can soak up through our taste buds and adrenals, rather than appreciate on our skin and from behind the Ray Bans. When the gray dampness forces us to the inside of the rain streaked window, we can look outside, and, with enough caffeine in our systems, actually believe we will not spend *next* summer doing anything but hiking, strolling the beaches, or getting that deck rebuilt.

With the coming of the indoor weather, the Avalon/Darkside Cinemas are gearing up for the busy season. The end of the Fall economic drought—that time when most businesses in Corvallis just eke by on lies to creditors and begging on street corners—means that the theaters will start filling up with refugees from the winter blues.

And yes, I did mention the Avalon. That's right, we are re-opening October 20th. Chances are, we will not have the liquor license nailed by then, but it won't be long. Frankly, the paperwork end of the licensing process feels like slow evisceration to me, so I wanna get the doors of the Avalon open and butts in the seats before I pop a couple Rolaids and cuss my way through the final stages. That means I need you, my kind and wise patrons, to come on down and see what we've done with the old gal. It's time to support the resurrection of the Avalon Cinema. And we will be giving you plenty of reason to do so.

We are opening the Avalon October 20th with CLEAR CUT: THE STORY OF PHILOMATH, OREGON. Local-boy-made-good Peter Richardson, who showed his documentary at Sundance Film Festival will be here to present his work and do a Q&A on Friday the 20th and Saturday the 21st. After the run of CLEAR CUT, we'll be bringing in RAISING FLAGG, a wonderful film made by Eugene filmmaker Neal Miller. He will come in and talk to you about what it's like to shoot a movie in Oregon with such stars as Alan Arkin and Lauren Holly.

From a fiscal standpoint, I'm relieved to see the rain-drenched reddening leaves out my kitchen window. That means I get to start paying bills again. Taking a little time off is in the cards, too. This weekend, we are heading to Bend for BendFilm, one of the best local film festivals in the state. Last year we got peeks at films that ended up in the Darkside: THE REAL DIRT ON FARMER JOHN and THE BEAUTY ACADEMY OF KABUL. So this year we hope to see more films worth bringing in to Corvallis. Is this time off, or am I working? Only my health care professionals know for sure, but it's still fun. John Waters is going to be at BendFilm and I hope to meet him and tell him the famous story about when we were playing his film PECKER at the Avalon Cinema.

Our downtown streets are filling up with students and I'm seeing orange and black everywhere. The temp is dropping at night, too. The heaters at the Avalon are in tip-top shape and ready to keep you cozy warm.

I have to say, this essay generated the most response. I have no idea why. We have many ways of not addressing our naughty, tingly, bulbous, no-no parts. Such euphemisms range from cute to down right disturbing. That degree of disturbing can be cubed if a baby voice is intoned while speaking it. Meanwhile, back in my childhood in the 60s and 70s, my mom's unique word was the life of the party. For that innocent time before a boy's voice changes to the point where vulgarities roll off the tongue, he has yet to possess a penis. Nope, it's anything but that.

Mom's Word For Penis

I was making a sign to discourage people from using their cell phones in the theater auditoriums. The first draft went a little like this:
WE ARE NOT IMPRESSED BY YOUR SENSE OF ENTITLEMENT AND IMPORTANCE. PLEASE SHUT OFF YOUR DAMNED CELL PHONE. My editor/wife/biz partner/best friend took a look at the sign and shook her head. Her comment: "Too hostile; don't be insulting, or if you do, at least make it funny. This presumes people are operating from a sense of entitlement instead of just plain forgetting."

I thought my sign was funny, and I couldn't care less about offending idiots who have developed such insulation from the feelings of others that they'll answer a call during a film. Those who just plain forgot to kill their phones would see the humor.

This whole sign thing had me thinking of the word "tronqus." (TRON-cuss) which was my mom's word for penis. When I shared that little childhood gem of a word with a friend, I thought he was going to rupture something with laughter. It wasn't so much the Beavis and Butthead "He said penis" guffaw, as it was the absurd sound of a word like tronqus. It could have been the word for bread crust, and he still would have laughed. Okay, we were teenagers. The fact that it was another word for penis really did make it funnier, as well as the echo of my mom saying it in her thick French-Canadian accent.

As we edged into our 20s, it became one of those words we could use to make each other laugh—especially at the most inappropriate times. If my buddy was playing the organ at church, I'd walk up and ask, "So, how's your tronqus?" There is nothing like watching someone trying to play Amazing Grace in front of the congregation while trying not to giggle. I'd be perched over the fender of an old Chevrolet, elbow deep in Quadrajet, and my buddy would spring the question, causing me to send tiny springs flying everywhere.

As with many car people, we had other car-nuts who would stop in. One such friend never got the hang of the tronqus thing. He would show up and ask, "How's your penis?" I'm guessing he didn't find the word tronqus as phonetically hilarious as we did and just didn't use it, no matter how many times we said, "Dude, you so don't get it." He probably thought it was a "naughty" thing, not a funny word thing. I'm sure he thought we had issues… or a relationship of some sort or other.

Ten years pass. My first wife and I were in Newport at the Wine & Seafood Festival. As we were pressing through the crowd, I heard someone behind me ask, "So, how's your penis?" My ex looked at me with her best who-the-hell-is-this look. Not an entirely inappropriate response to someone asking, perhaps a little too loudly, after her husband's genitalia. I promptly corrected my old friend whom I hadn't seen in a decade, and who still didn't get it.

"It's tronqus. Asking about someone's penis isn't funny."

A girl walking by, obviously enjoying more wine than seafood, chimed in: "Actually, I think it's real funny!"

Meanwhile, my then-wife was looking at me with raised eyebrows, waiting for something to chase away the questions in her mind. I was thinking, this would be a dandy time to be struck dead with lightening. Not a cloud in the sky. I tried explaining to my ex how this was an old joke. She wasn't buying it.

Asking about someone's penis, unless it is caught in a bear trap and you are trying to release it, just ain't cool. But asking about someone's tronqus, well, it just doesn't get better than that.

I know there are people who will unsubscribe from this email newsletter because I used the P-word, since being forced to consider such things is not their cup of tea. Others will roll their eyes, mumble "Oh, *Paul*," and hope I do a little better next week. Still others will find it very funny, and will forward it to their friends… and I will see a surge in email sign-ups. There will always be those who lack the social flexibility to embrace the humor that skulks beneath the crude crust of some of my more inappropriate wit. But the best response will be from those who send me the story of their own personal "tronqus" word. Many of you have stories much better than mine.

Meanwhile, back to the point of all of this: The world is full of literal people. They are the ones who will think the tronqus joke is about male anatomy, when in fact it is about the aural hilarity of the word, accented by the lengths we'll go as a species to not directly discuss things related to sex.

Many will see my cell signage as hostile to innocently forgetful mobile phone users—disrespecting anyone, including me, who might forget to turn their phone to vibrate. In fact, I'm disrespecting those possessing that special degree of ass-holiness that compels them to actually *answer* a cell phone during a movie and then *talk*.

So, I will rewrite my signage for the more literal and sensitive patrons. I will also steel myself against the emails telling me how unfunny this essay is, and that I need to find another place to work out my sexual fantasies/issues, passive aggressiveness, and to just grow the hell up. (As my wife said when she read the first draft of this, "And next year, you'll be twelve!") And in my response to those literal and sensitive readers, I will endeavor to not be a tronqus.

Coda: Response to Tronqus

Fears of having offended you with last week's column were quickly staved off by my receiving the most humorous responses ever to one of my email newsletters. You people are funnier than I could ever hope to be. Almost all of you thought my cell phone usage sign was far too tame. Those who took the time to recount stories of humorous-sounding words made my day. But I have to say that nothing compares to the moment the little old lady passing me on the street asked, "Hey, how's your tronqus?"

It's Oregon. The weather we have here sucks, even for those who have been here for a long time. There is no way to explain to the uninitiated that going from a California winter to an Oregon winter is like going from a three-pack-a-day cigarette habit to one pack of peppermint sugarless gum... per week. When faced with a sugarless gum winter, I think of the heat in Sacramento, which I hate marginally more than sloppy, seeping rain that can ooze through every seam of my raincoat.

Rain and the Indian

When the weather goes to rainy gray, and outdoor activity is limited to running from the car to the door and back with collars turned up and hats pulled down, Seasonal Affective Disorder is a very real downer that moves in like a big-assed rain cloud ruining your psychic picnic. I suffer from S.A.D. but mine hits during the brightest part of the summer, when the movie season typically grinds to a painful, slow crawl. I get depressed about having to lie, borrow money, and dodge landlords until the rains hit. So, as the sun sets on prime motorcycling weather, I'm trying to ignore the few sunrays that are left, while appeasing the wolves at the gate. It's enough to send Gandhi on a killing spree.

For my odd psyche, there is a certain peace that comes with the winter rains. Someone (maybe Tom Robbins?) once said of the NW climate, "The weather outside matches my internal climate." I stir to consciousness in my bed watching hissing droplets bounce off the roof out my window, as my cat gently pulls my hand into his chest with clingy claws, and licks the hair on my knuckles. Coffee tastes better and the weight of the winter comforter might as well be shackles for the difficulty it causes me getting out of bed. The rains mean I can go into my garage and not purposely ignore my motorcycle, who is listing on her sidestand wondering why it's been weeks since she roared. I can tell her it's raining, not that I'm too busy for her.

When it comes to trying to turn the lemon rains of winter into lemonade, nothing works like the memory of 107 Middle-of-nowhere-Wyoming degrees.

I had been riding all day trying to make it to Sheridan, Wyoming, to rendezvous with a buddy coming in from Illinois. The day bore the kind of heat so intense I had to soak my T-shirt at every rest stop faucet, and, after 10 minutes of riding, not only was it dry, it was stiff from minerals. I was drinking a liter of water an hour and knew it wasn't enough, but the water at the rest stops was only good for soaking shirts. It was the worst part of the afternoon, when the heat was apexing and my mood and humor bottoming out. I pulled into a gas station, and, after gassing up, headed inside the western motif store/restaurant for food and more water. This was reservation country. The Native Americans seemed pretty detached from the white folks wandering around inside—the whites not knowing the difference between this tourist trap and the real west.

There is a thing that happens when you spend a lot of time in the saddle and cover a lot of geography. A hardening of manner prevails, combined with a sharpening of reflexes that comes from dealing with the hailstorm of rocks, tire parts, and weather hurling over the windscreen into your face. Many people wonder what kind of cognitive slippage makes one consider this a vacation. The answer is that traveling by motorcycle peels away the layers of codependence. After a few weeks of living on the road, you do not give a shit who you offend or frighten. There is freedom in that—a release, if you will, that constitutes a real vacation. In reality, the tough-guy crap is quickly traded for ambassadorship when someone asks about the bike, the ride, or wants to tell you about the Harley they rode after the war—any war. You count on these drivers not to kill you, so you are nice to them.

But this day there was heat. I was feeling antisocial. In the booth in front of me were a native man and his wife, both with skin toughened by years of sun, speaking their native language. The white folk were staring like the Indians were some sort of museum display. I was minding my own business looking at a map while I splattered it with mayo. The Indian man with the leather face looked over at me with a, "Hey?"

I was not in the mood to interact with anyone. So I silently looked up at him.

"Where ya from?" sez he. Oh, great. Now all the sweaty tourists were looking at me, too.

"Oregon." He took off the hat he was wearing and showed me it was from the Pendleton Round-Up.

"I rode in the Round-Up more years than I care to admit."

"Nice country out there." Now, let me get back to my damn sandwich and map. But he doesn't stop.

"Where you headin'?"

I closed my map with a little too much drama and looked at him, then at the shifting crowd waiting for my answer.

"Tryin' to get to Sheridan for the night."

Beat.

"I'm gonna tell you where to stay there." Lucky me. "There's the main drag. I forget what it's called. But there's a hotel on it. It's white, I think."

"That narrows it right down."

"Now, hold on. You'll know it when you see it. Ya know why?" The suspense was killing me. "Because there's a big white limo in front of it."

The crowd chuckled. I was hoping this was the punch line.

"And why the hell should I stay there?"

"Because the folks there (he looked around the restaurant) *ain't white.*"

The crowd of eavesdroppers quickly cleared its collective throats and found somewhere else to look. I laughed. My strain of native blood is pretty lean, but I've had more than a couple people pick me out of a crowd. The old guy winked at me.

"They're good Indians." Alrighty, then.

With a water-soaked T-shirt, full gas tank, and stabilized blood sugar, I hit the road. In a few hours I was in Sheridan and met my buddy, who'd arrived only 15 miraculous minutes earlier from as far east as I had come west. We feasted at a Chinese buffet and I told him we needed to find this certain motel. One of the reasons Monty and I travel so well together is that he doesn't need a lot of convincing. We pulled up next to a rather unimpressive establishment graced with a seemingly inappropriate but, yes—white—limousine. Shortly after I stepped inside, Monty could hear me laughing all the way out in the parking lot. The "Good Indians" were East Indians, not Native Americans. The old guy'd set me up hundreds of miles ago, even though he'd never see the punch line.

My cat goes to sleep with a furry sigh and his claws retract from my skin. Slowly I take my hand back and slip out of bed. I'm thinking: the weather sucks. I'll write something about a summer ride. People might get a smile and a memory of their own summer joy. And it might help them forget about those beautiful leaves we will all soon need to slop out of our gutters.

We were a crew of three guys who had three days to clear out all the seats in the Harbor Theater. The owner wanted them gone and offered them for the bottom basement price of free. When it comes to theater seats, there is no such thing as free. We had to unbolt them from the floor, where they'd been for decades. Theater seats are heavy and take up a lot of space. We had to rent the biggest Budget Rental truck we could find. Then once we got them home, they had to be cleaned. This ain't cheap and is far from fun. Then they had to be stored until the Darkside was ready to have them installed. Well, not quite. The months spent in storage were unkind, and they needed to be cleaned again. Double happiness. Of the 300 seats we unbolted, about half went into the landfill. We lost half again when they were cleaned the second time. So, once the smoke cleared, we'd spent a fair amount on each "free" seat.

The Harbor Theater in Florence

The Harbor Theater was a cute little single-screen that served the coastal community for years on the waterfront of Florence, Oregon. The quaintness of a small-town theater couldn't compete with the building of a chain multiplex nearby, so the owners turned the Harbor Theater over, and it was destined to become retail space. Like a vulture picking at the bones of the old cinema, I spent several days taking out the vintage Heywood Wakefield seats from the old auditorium, reducing the space to a terraced concrete expanse. We moved the seats out the rear door to avoid contact with the locals, who felt a certain sense of ownership in the old icon, and who might consider our gravedigger's tactics worthy of a sturdy tongue-lashing.

While poking around the building I found the perfectly aged theater sign collecting dust in the boiler room, retired from her place hanging from the high front of the building. The owner wouldn't sell it to me, even after I cleared out all the seats, and bought the ice machine and popcorn machine.

The Harbor seats ended up in the Darkside after a thorough cleaning. Months later, I had a rare day off, so I pulled the motorcycle out of the garage and headed west for a lazy ride. I hit Florence in the afternoon and settled in with a cup of coffee and a view of the bridge. I let the sun warm my leathers as I sipped and read the local paper. Not a bad way to blow an afternoon.

With a certain apprehension, I decided to see how the conversion of the Harbor Theater had finished up. They had done a nice job turning it into a shoe store, leveling the floor and putting in skylights. As I poked around, a nice young woman asked if she could help me. I asked what happened to the old theater sign that was rotting in the old boiler room. She told me her dad was taking it to the dump that very day. I begged her to call her dad.

After she handed me the phone, he explained that he'd asked historical societies and museums to take it and all had declined, so he had it loaded into the back of his truck for disposal. I told him that I was on a motorcycle that day, making it a tad unhandy to cart a ten-foot sign home, but I would give it a good home if he would let me come back for it. He told me to be there with a van by 9:00 a.m. the next day or it would be landfill. When I pulled my old van into his driveway the next morning, I could see the old sign with its well-earned patina, resting on its side in the gravel. It was too long to fit in the back of my van, which made for a drafty ride home with the back hatch open.

The original Harbor Theater sign now lives in its place of honor, in the lower lobby of the Darkside. No more pelting with rain and salt air, just dust and curious fingers. A replica made of stainless steel adorns the front of the old Harbor Theater over the door of the shoe store, so far holding its promise to never rot and tarnish.

When I don't want to leave my big black motorcycle on the street while I work, I sometimes park it in the lower lobby next to the big theater sign. It adds a nice punctuation to the story if someone asks me where that grand old sign came from.

The Whiteside Theater was built in 1922 as a cinema. It was built in Italian Renaissance style and showed movies for about 80 years before the doors closed for good in 2002. This theater is an emotional epicenter for the city of Corvallis, where the empty theater still stands in the center of the old downtown. The building has been closed for about five years, as of this writing. That half-decade has not been kind to her. There is now an effort underway to acquire and restore the building. Some believe there is hope for the building to once again be a moving picture palace. Others, not so much. I might be considered on the not-so-much side of this. This has put me in the crosshairs.

The Whiteside Theater

W ith the future of the Whiteside Theater on everyone's minds, I am frequently asked to weigh in. *Why* I'm asked eludes me, but I'm still asked. I recently rediscovered my ticket stub from the last show of the Whiteside ("Ohhhhh, my Precious…"). Somehow I had sensed that 2002 was going to be the final year for the 900-seat venue, and slipped the ticket into the back of my desk drawer.

Now, more than four years later, people are asking me what we can do with the old architectural beauty on one of the prime downtown intersections. I suggest we turn it into a Scientology, Jews-for-Jesus, Muslim, non-profit, tax-exempt, parolee halfway house, heroin drug rehab center, homeless shelter with a five star restaurant upstairs and a Wal-Mart in the west wall. The marquee could be changed out for one of those animated LED affairs advertising the basement casino, and we could put a frat house on the roof. We all know a functioning sewage system is overrated, so let's just line Madison and 4th with neon blue Port-a-Potties again, and while we're at it, let's reserve some of that frontage for the new Graffiti Wall. Oh, and make double-damn sure all the materials for such extensive remodeling have been purchased from our new Home Depot, and not our locally owned community treasure, Robnett's Hardware.

At the risk of not being silly, I must tell you that the Whiteside is simply not financially viable as a movie theater. Pardon the immodesty, but I would know. And since I'm also on the board of the Majestic Theater, I have an opinion or two about what it's like to run a live venue in this town. So, if you rule out cinema and a performance venue, what do you have left? Your memories of exploring heterosexuality on the Whiteside balcony while Indiana Jones dodges Nazis will not pay the bills, and will not excite investors to pay them, either.

Frankly, I will be a wreck when they start whatever transformation takes place at the Whiteside. I've spent 30 years as an exhibitor, and watching one old venue after another become road-kill on the digital entertainment highway doesn't do me a lot of good. And just like you, I have personal memories of seeing movies at the Whiteside with my family. But how I feel about the old queen does not change the way business works. And that sucks.

From the roof of the Lipmann building, the building that houses the greatness that is the Darkside Cinema, we can see the roof of the Whiteside Theater and the large hole that allows water to stream into the plaster interior of the auditorium. Such a dumping of water is eroding the old movie palace.

In the 1990s, my friend JohnBarnes was the manager of both the Whiteside and the 11 parking spaces that—back then—were the State Theater. (We called John "JohnBarnes" because everyone said his first name and last name like it was one word. Even since he got married, and he and his wife took on a unique surname, we still call him JohnBarnes.) JohnBarnes is a tall, lean kid with dark hair, frequently mistaken as my son due to his startling good looks. A more pronounced similarity was our love of movie theaters. He had the good fortune to run the Whiteside and I had the good fortune to be his friend, so when the crowds let out, we would sometimes crawl about the old building, exploring the catwalks and closets within closets.

JohnBarnes was a great tour guide. Once, he showed me the original curtains that had adorned the old vaudeville house. I admit I rescued them, mouse-eaten and filthy, from the dumpster when they were tossed out. He knew it was against policy to actually hand me items from the theater as they did a major cleanout, so JohnBarnes would just call me and say it was a lovely night to dumpster dive. A Regal executive strolled through the Avalon one day and noted some of the Whiteside paraphernalia. Instead of challenging me, he just nodded. As the months went by, certain theater antiquities started "anonymously" appearing on my doorstep, saved from the landfill. The "State" sign letters in the Avalon were "liberated" from the wrecking site by a local resident. Even the little wooden and wire stool presently residing in the Darkside Cinema lobby was at the original 1922 opening of the Whiteside.

The woman's face set into the façade of the Whiteside building seems to be glowering down on Madison Avenue, a wee pissed that we abandoned the building behind her to gather around our glass (now plasma) screens at home and let her rot. You see, back in the day, before CNN was in every airport and Fox News provided a platform for the conservative cant, the Whiteside was where Corvallis got her news with moving pictures. That's right, they were the pre-show newsreels. There's a CINEMA PARADISO-ish charm to picturing the community coming together in front of a flickering screen to see the bombing of Pearl Harbor, or Grace Kelly's wedding to Prince Rainier. Imagine our city watching the events of 9/11 unfold on the curved screen of the Whiteside, all 900 seats filled with gasping souls shocked by images of terrorism on our soil. Images they had not seen moving until that moment. This is the emotional, the true emotional history of the Whiteside. People experienced the outside world in this building. These days, my cell phone can play the uncensored video of the Michael Richards tirade. Back before TV, if you wanted moving pictures, film was it. Though the racism was institutionally condoned back when the Whiteside was showing newsreels, such language as we hear today in even PG-13 fare would have been off limits. Today, she is closed and we don't get any less news because of it.

Let's look a little more closely at the closure of the Whiteside. The building is, at least as of this writing, owned by Regal Cinemas—the biggest cinema chain in the world: "...consisting of 6,383 screens in 542 theatres in 40 states as of June 29, 2006, with over 244 million annual attendees for the fiscal year ended December 29, 2005" (according to www.regalcinemas.com). So, with all that, why did the Whiteside have to close?

Toward the end of 2001, Regal Cinemas declared Chapter 11 bankruptcy with about $2 billion in debt, almost all of that from building too many cinemas too fast. So, when it came time to trim up, which do you think they were going to close down: the more profitable gigaplexes or the struggling single screens?

Frankly, even if we had made the Whiteside more profitable than the Regal Ninth Street Cinema, they still would have had to close it, because with the coming of the Carmike 12-plex, the four-screen Ninth Street stood the best chance of keeping Regal in the Corvallis cinema game. Since the local powers bought the bullshit that the Carmike 12-plex was going to also be a "conference center" (their way of skirting the zoning issues), Carmike was free to come into a community that already had enough screens to satisfy the movie-going population.

The reality is, the Ninth Street Cinema was doing poorly mostly due to the crappy presentation. More than once I walked into the projection booth to adjust the picture, since the projectionist there couldn't find the framing knob. They would destroy prints and keep playing them. The help raised apathy to an art form, and the constant turnover of managers did nothing to get things back on track. So, any person who had the power to approve the coming of Carmike would have no trouble doing so after their Ninth Street Cinema experience. A new theater would serve the community better than what Regal was doing. However, it wouldn't have taken a rocket scientist to figure out the town didn't need a 12-plex.

The numbers do not crunch kindly for the Whiteside Theater. To open it as a cinema again, there is probably about a million dollars in work to make the building habitable. That's before the doors can open. Add to that $500,000 needed to buy the building and you have payments that will never come close to being met by a single screen theater in a 50k population town with 21 screens.

So, how about opening it as a live venue with food? This is where things get really fun. If you make the Whiteside something other than a theater you get hit with federal, state, county, and city "change of use" requirements.

Let's start with parking. Right now the old gal's parking is grandfathered in. As soon as you make her something other than a cinema, you need to comply with all the parking requirements as new construction.

Then we have seismic requirements. As she sits, you can open her as a cinema (after renovation) and get away with everything pretty much as it is. Make it a restaurant or nightclub, and you'll need to cover every brick wall with chain link (during a seismic event, the shifting of the building will compress the bricks so they spit out like killer watermelon seeds). That balcony will probably have to go, and we're not even warmed up yet.

So let's say you get all new plumbing, heating, cooling, roof, electrical, projection equipment, restrooms and so on, and, presto, you're open as a cinema. Did you think you would be able to get films? Any movie company that even thinks of giving the Whiteside a movie that would fill the 900 seats will get three kinds of hell from Carmike. If Fine Line Features discovers Tolkein wrote another Lord of the Rings and gives that movie to the Whiteside, they can pretty much count on Carmike not playing any of their other films for a long time—and not just in Corvallis. It's Show Business, kids. Not Show Art. Fine Line will make the smart business decision. End of story.

Old films have their fan base here, but won't draw 900 people a night in this town. Trust me. I know. The art-house market would be a lawnmower engine trying to propel the Whiteside locomotive.

No matter what happens with the Whiteside, I'll always have my memories of climbing through the building with JohnBarnes like we were a couple of little kids, just as you will have *your* Whiteside memories. No matter what happens at the corner of 4th and Madison, whether it becomes parking spaces like the State, or a ward of the state, when we stand on the roof of the Book Bin building, we'll be looking down on the next chapter of Corvallis history. Some will like it. Some will not. That does nothing to diminish the memories we take with us into our personal futures.

When I travel alone I tend to disconnect from the comforts most people seem to find necessary, like showers, clean clothes, and social graces. When I travel with some of my long-term biker buddies, this austerity ethic is the norm. Traveling outside of the usual comforts tends to invite a spirit of spontaneity and unpredictability. One never quite knows what or whom they'll run into next. Remembrances of rides and subsequent ridiculousness tend to sustain me through the crappy winter Oregon weather when it seems all I do is move from one showtime to the next, unencumbered by anything resembling spontaneity.

Yellowstone Nudity

Yellowstone had been closed for a few days due to wildfires, so the regatta of RVs and minivans, well-stocked with families, was choking the roads through the park. The advantage of motorcycling through Yellowstone is that one can creep around the lumbering aluminum Winnies, rather than getting stuck behind their ample behinds as they slow down to look at what you'd think was the world's only deer. The drawback of motorcycling through Yellowstone is that the roaming buffalo are huge mobile walls of meat that wander around the place like they were there first.

Monty and I were on our way to see Old Faithful do that thing she does. The crowds were thick and she wasn't set to blow for some time, so we found a spot away from the masses and settled in to wait. Monty pulled out his pipe, a long-stemmed affair that made him look a bit like an olde English pub owner, and I had my bottle of water, which made me look like I was from the NW.

With no invitation and even less warning, a woman wandered into our space. Being that I'm kind of hard to miss and Monty is roughly the size of a small planet, I'm guessing it was the way we were resting silently, draped over a couple of rough-cut log benches, that rendered us invisible to her. We knew she'd missed seeing the roughly 500 pounds of leather-clad bikers dozing behind her, because she proceeded to remove and adjust the wrap around her waist with a speed that didn't allow for a cautionary "sweetheart-you-ain't-alone" throat-clearing.

Very quickly it became apparent she was "going commando": sans panties. After retying her skirt, she looked up and saw Monty and me, lounging about ten feet away. Monty nonchalantly nodded to her, as if to say, "Nice day."

Instead of screaming like we'd ambushed her in the women's changing room at Nordstrom, she smiled politely, as if to say, "Yes, it's lovely," and walked off. Monty removed his pipe from his mouth, blew out some smoke, and said to no one in particular, "You know, life is good."

As we traveled to the west end of the park, we spotted a herd of elk. It was moving in our direction, so we stopped and seated ourselves at the top of the slope leading down to a stream, which Monty had guessed correctly was their destination. The elk gracefully wandered into the water, and soon more and more people were gathering around us to watch the wild animals bathe and graze.

With no ceremony, a young man broke from the crowd and headed down the slope toward the herd. Monty speculated this person was either going to spook the herd or discover elk are not domesticated. The man slowly approached the shore of the stream. The elk were watching him like he was wearing a pink sheet to a Klan meeting—not at all amused. Then the man slowly removed every stitch of his clothing. Exercising his gift for understatement, "Not much of an antler," was all Monty said. The crowd around us chuckled nervously.

The man very casually wandered into the middle of the herd and lowered himself into the water. Interestingly enough, the elk seemed to lose interest in him and went about their elk business. For about twenty minutes, the man silently communed with the herd as we watched, wondering if the herd was going to take exception to the human and violently defend their stream. The human herd on the side of the road grew, about half being newcomers not realizing we were watching a nude man in the water more than the indigenous wildlife.

Slowly the man stood up and made his way to the shore, regaining the attention of the herd, and some gasps from the unsuspecting latecomers. He dressed, bowed to the attentive herd, and walked away toward the crowd. As he passed between Monty and me, sitting on separate logs, he looked over at me without stopping, and asked, "How's it goin'?"

Monty's comment: "Old boyfriend?"

I pointedly stated I had no idea who this guy was. Monty just shook his head and relit his pipe. The crowd thinned and the herd moved back into the woods. Ahh, the wildlife.

It's the rain, you know. When it hits, I start time traveling back to summer rides and the things that can only happen when sun and motorcycles occupy the same space at the same time. The feedback I get from you about these stories has been great. Even as I feel a certain guilt for not pontificating exclusively about biz, my blundering, typing fingers are seized by the spirit of motorcycling stories. I send this weekly email to literally thousands of people, and few of you are shy about giving feedback, so I figure I'm good to go. And if you've been over there thinking, "He's just not business-like enough," I promise next week to include shameless plugs for Avalon/Darkside memberships, gift certificates, and T-shirts for your holiday shopping.

Coda, from the next week's email:

Many people responded to my story about riding through Yellowstone. Thank you. More than a few of you pointed out my wimpiness by telling your own tales of riding bicycles through these rugged areas. It reminded me of when Monty and I were at a store that teetered on the continental divide. We'd been riding most of the day and had stopped to eat and rest. As we leaned over the rail of the fence overlooking the road, a couple of bicyclists came by. Since we were at about 10,000 feet, this was actually pretty impressive. The guy next to us asked, with a thick New York accent, "What the hell do you say to people like that? You know they gotta be nuts."

Monty looked up and said, "I say, 'thank you.' Because of them I know by the time I ride by, the bears have been fed."

What follows are a series of Frequently Asked Questions that I began writing and collecting when I was building my first theater, the Avalon Cinema, in 1996. I was converting an old truck garage into a single-screen, 100-seat art cinema in Corvallis, Oregon. As in any small town, word traveled fast and people stopped by throughout the day to peer in, trying to see what kind of crazy person would try a stunt like this. Each person asked some variation on the same questions. As much as I appreciated the interest, it made it hard to get anything done. In an effort to stop the curious at the front window, I began posting what I hoped were the answers to many of the questions the passersby wanted to ask. Putting them in print allowed me to resume swinging a hammer in relative peace.

FAQs

FAQs (July 1997)

Q: What is the Avalon Cinema?
A: It's a building about 50 by 60 feet.

Q: What will it be showing?
A: Movies.

Q: What kind of movies?
A: Art, foreign, and alternative films. If you are familiar with the International Film Series at OSU, we will be paralleling their programming. Also, we'll show the stuff I like and maybe some of what you suggest.

Q: Like what?
A: We'll see. So far major suggestions seem to be: gay and lesbian films, Bogart, Peter Sellers, directors' cuts of older films, and the works of various directors.

Q: Will you show porno films?
A: Not a chance in hell.

Q: When will you be open?
A: God knows. Say, around the end of June.

Q: This year? (1997)
A: It's looking like it.

Q: When will you be showing movies?
A: From 6:00 p.m. Monday through Saturday. Starting noon on Sunday.

Q: How big is your screen?
A: I could park my '62 Impala on it and not have a tire on the ground (12 by 22 feet).

Q: Will you have THX Dolby surround sound?
A: Are you on drugs? I can't afford that! Believe it or not, for decades theaters had fantastic sound before the digital age. So will we.

Q: What will you be selling in your snack bar?
A: Food and drink, mostly.

Q: No, really.
A: OK, fresh, fat-filled popcorn until enough people whine, and then I'll get in some bagged air-popped crap. Canned and bottled drinks, so we don't have to deal with the complexities of serving real food. Feel free to make suggestions.

Q: Will you have air conditioning?
A: The jury's still out on that one. If I can't make things comfortable without it, then we'll see what I can do.

Q: Are you accepting applications?
A: Not at this time. I have a partner and three kids I have to put to work before I can hire anyone else. Feel free to ask after we've been open for a while.

Q: How many seats will you have?
A: 73.

Q: Are they comfortable?
A: If you are exactly average size, they are. Well, maybe not.

Q: Will you allow smoking?
A: Only if you are on fire.

Q: Do you plan to serve alcohol?
A: Maybe sometime in the future if enough people show interest. Right now I still have to prove I am not the anti-Christ, so I will not be applying for an OLCC permit for quite some time.

Q: Will you be showing very old movies?
A: We will have 35mm equipment. Many of the older titles are on 16mm film, so there lies our limitations.

Q: Tell me about your rest rooms?
A: No.

Q: Is a dog's mouth really cleaner than a human's?
A: I sincerely doubt it.

Q: What if a question I have isn't answered here?
A: E-mail me, or call. Or, you can try sticking your head in the door and see if I'm around. (By the way, if you make me come down from the scaffolding to try to sell me something, I will be grumpy.) But, I am always willing to take a minute and answer questions—as long as the task I'm doing allows me to pause. Thank you for the support and encouragement so many of you have shown.

More FAQs (August 1997)

After the first FAQs were posted on the glass of the Avalon's front door, people wanted more. It wasn't until we had been open a while that I put up the second set.

Q: Why do you post these questions?
Short answer: My door. I'll use it how I want.

Long answer: Because I'm pretty much working alone, I often am doing tasks that cannot be bookmarked. So, by reading these, with any luck you will have some of your questions answered without having to put up with my pissy attitude. This new one is due to frequently asked questions not covered in the old FAQ sheet.

Q: So, it's the end of June. Why are you not opened?
Short answer: 'Cause.
Long answer: In each life there is a certain amount of uncertainty. Often events and complications occur that cannot be avoided, thus prolonging anticipated events. In other words, because I ain't got all the work done yet.

Q: So when will you be open, then?
Short answer: Yes.
Long answer: Since we have agreed to host the da Vinci Days Animation Festival, it would be right handy to be open by the middle of July. Since the da Vinci Days people have the power to help expedite "things" the middle of July is looking very good.

Q: Why are you opening this theater?
Short answer: I'm in it for the babes.
Long answer: I'm in it for the money.

Q: Really?
Short answer: No.
Long answer: Nope.

Q: If this door is open, can I come in?
Short answer: If I'm expecting you.
Long answer: If I'm not busy, I'd love to answer questions. If you don't know construction site etiquette, don't come tromping in. You might get hurt, or worse yet, hurt me. (The rudest thing I've had happen so far is someone tapping me on the shoulder while I was cutting plywood with a power saw. He never got a chance to tell me what he wanted. The police are still investigating, so don't tell. That's when the barricade went up.)

Q: Is there anything I can do to help you get opened sooner?
Short answer: Slip tens and twenties under the door.
Long answer: No, but thank you for asking. The best thing anyone can do for any new business is get the word out and make suggestions on how YOU think this place should be run. Even if I laugh at you.

Q: I want to know how much tickets are going to be!
Short answer: That's nice.
Long answer: Ticket prices are not some arbitrary number I pick out of my head like I'm playing the lottery. It will be based on what this place needs to gross to pay the bills. That number cannot be calculated until more inspections have been passed. At this time it's hovering around five bucks a head for full-priced shows. I suspect I'll also apply a sliding scale based on how much I like you. See old FAQ sheet, too.

Q: Who writes your material?
Short answer: A small troll who lives in the rafters.
Long answer: The guy you'll be giving your money to when you come here to spend lots of it.

Still more FAQs (September 1997)

Q: What is the Avalon Cinema?
Evil Paul: A monstrous pain in the…
Good Paul: Upon completion, it will be a small art cinema showing foreign, alternative, and independent films.

Q: What kind of films will you show?
Evil Paul: Movies that don't dive into the cesspool of mediocrity with their mouths wide open.
Good Paul: If you are familiar with the International Film Series at OSU, you have a good idea of what our core programming will be. If the product is available, I'd like to augment that with works of various directors, favorite actors, and really bad biker movies. I might even think about what you suggest.

Q: What has been suggested?

Evil Paul: Do you know how hard it is to keep a straight face while someone is telling you how much they'd like to see...

Good Paul: The diversity of suggested films has been amazing. It seems the most popular requests have been gay and lesbian films, Kubrick movies, Peter Sellers films, and even some of the better Clint Eastwood films (and no, that's not oxymoronical).

Q: When will the Avalon be open?

Evil Paul: When it's done.

Good Paul: August.

Q: You have given opening dates before that have come and gone, and yet you are still under construction. What's the deal?

Evil Paul: What the hell do you think I'm doing in here? Drinking beer and watching Sally? These calluses aren't from...

Good Paul: I am sorry about the delays, but the best-laid plans can be upset by failed inspections and cost over-runs. Seeing how this is basically a one-man operation, things are going as well as possible.

Q: How much will it be for tickets?

Evil Paul: Divide the number of times I've been asked that question by your gross annual income and you'll be close.

Good Paul: The price for a ticket is based on what it costs to keep the payments up on the construction loans and keep the rent paid. It is not some arbitrary number that looks good on the reader board. At this time, it is hovering around five bucks a head with cheaper matinees on Sunday.

Q: Some one said you would be showing porno movies.

Evil Paul: Not a chance in hell.

Good Paul: Not a damn chance in hell.

Q: Will you have air conditioning?

Evil Paul: No. We'll just hand out towels and charge an extra five dollars a head for the sauna.

Good Paul: I am currently making a deal on a swamp cooler which will make it quite comfortable on the hot days.

Q:	Tell me about your snack bar.
Evil Paul:	No.
Good Paul:	We'll start by serving stuff I like. Then, as your suggestions and threats accumulate, I'll make changes. For now, glorious fat-filled popcorn (served with a stethoscope so you can listen to your arteries harden while you eat it) and canned and bottled pop, juices, and cold coffee drinks. We will have goodies for those who worry about their fat intake (you know, those incapable of living a little when they go out). A sugar buzz will be offered with the variety changing frequently.

Q:	Are you accepting applications?
Evil Paul:	Only if you work for free and call me "Supreme Ruler of the Universe."
Good Paul:	Not at this time. Ask when we have been open a spell. If you bring me a resume when I'm working on this place, I promise to lose it.

Q:	How many seats will you have?
Evil Paul:	Just the one God gave me.
Good Paul:	The auditorium will seat 73. Sixty-nine will be fixed and a space with four movable seats will be available for wheel chair parking.

Q:	Are they comfortable?
Evil Paul:	Compared to what?
Good Paul:	What we lack in head rests and cup holders we make up for in legroom.

Q:	Will you allow smoking?
Evil Paul:	Only if I light you on fire.
Good Paul:	No. But, we'll let you run outside to puff a fag with only minor harassment when you try to come back in.

Q:	Will you serve beer?
Evil Paul:	Only to the employees.
Good Paul:	In the future we may apply for an OLCC permit to serve beer. At this time we have no plans to do so.

Q:	Are you going to be showing old movies?
Evil Paul:	Only if I like 'em.
Good Paul:	If they are available. Email me, call, or slip me a note telling me what you wanna see.

Q:	Why are you opening this theater?
Evil Paul:	I'm in it for the babes.
Good Paul:	I'm in it for the money.

Q:	Really?
Evil Paul:	Like I'm going to admit it…
Good Paul:	Nope.

Newer FAQs (May 1998)

Q: Do you allow dogs in your theater?

A: My dog can frequently be found lounging on the stairs up to the booth or in front of the lobby sofa (older Australian Shepherd). However, my dog biting someone is about as likely as Clinton taking a vow of celibacy. Also, my dog will not wander into the snack bar area, and my wife is usually here to watch her, so I don't have to touch her (the dog) while I'm working. I have let customers with lap dogs in for the movie (on very slow nights), after they swear on a stack of Gideons that they will not let the animal's feet touch the ground and that if it barks once, it's back out to the car. I would really think twice before allowing two dogs in at the same time. There are some people who are allergic to animals, so I keep that in mind whenever someone asks if they can bring their dog in.

Q: What happened to the small popcorn cups? Why bags?

A: In our undying concern for the environment, we changed over to the recyclable paper bags. The real reason: Popcorn prices go up in the summer like gas prices (summer movies mean more people buying popcorn). It was a choice between raising prices or going to a cheaper container. The price will go up 50 cents in the future, but this should hold it for a spell.

Q: Are all your movies going to run two weeks?

A: We are getting to a comfort level with the movie companies where we can book a movie for a week with the option to go two if it takes off (or "has legs," to use theater-speak). Often we have a damned good movie, but the turnout is low. So, when I know there are more people out there to see it I'll hold it over and whine at the Avalon-ites to get their butts in here. In the real world, this means half the shipping charges, and I don't have to spend my Friday building up and tearing down film.

Q: Your women's room was very cold in the winter.
A: You're right, it was.

Q: Are you hiring?
A: I have two 16 year-old daughters who have allowances to earn. Our seating capacity keeps that to about all the help I need. However, if you walked in and knew how to run movie projectors...

Q: Why don't you train someone to run projectors?
A: Any chimp can learn to thread a projector. It's knowing what to do when something goes wrong that makes a projectionist. You have to be pretty anal retentive to keep the system clean and running at its peak. Since the distance from the screen to the projector is short, the image can very easily go out of focus as the glass (lens) warms up. Finding people who are mechanical and on the ball enough to make sure the presentation is as good as it can be, is a little tricky.

Q: Are you going to make it?
A: Jury's still out on that one.

Q: Sometimes it seems as though the image is flickering more than it should be.
A: Big bulb, close to screen. When we show a Cinemascope picture, (Kundun, Hindi movies) you'll notice no flickering. Still working on getting it gone from the flat movies.

Q: Why is it cool in your auditorium?
A: Because I'm not. Tell me it's cool and I'll do something about it. Say nothing and the temp stays where it's comfy for me.

Q: Sometimes it seems the image is out of focus.

A: Sometimes it is. Since I check the film a dozen or so times during the presentation, it is rarely my fault. More often than not, it's the cinematographer. I just about went nuts during Mrs. Brown because she would be "soft" but the wallpaper pattern behind her would be tack sharp. Nothing I can do about that.

Q: When will you have beer?

A: I'm having one now.

Even more FAQs (August 1999)

Q: Thought you were going to close for the summer?

A: See, that's what happens when you think too much. Actually, between having a hired gun getting me real movies and being discovered by the senior citizen set, we managed to stay open. No complaints. Plus, we are grateful that "Star Wars" sucked.

Q: Why don't you switch early and late shows every day so people who work late or get up early can see both features?

A: Do you know how much trouble we have with the shows at the same time every night? People still can't figure it out. Chaos would reign. The world as we know it would change. And we don't want that.

Q: Why do I have so much trouble understanding the dialogue on films where the actors have accents?

A: Because you are ethnocentric. You believe that everyone should speak exactly as you do. When you free yourself of the chains of prejudice, all will be clear. Really. We guarantee it. Okay, maybe not. Maybe the dialogue tracks on some prints have been pretty bad. Maybe I'm thinking seriously about going to digital sound which may or may not help. Maybe this is a plot by the distributors of the movies to get all us analogue houses to convert to digital. Maybe very soon they will be making prints with no analogue tracks at all, so making them perfect isn't as important as it used to be. Maybe I need to move on to the next question.

Q: Why is it so hot in your theater?

111

A: Because it's hot outside. Duh. OK, because air conditioning is expensive and I might need to go to digital sound, which we will use 12 months out of the year, making it a much better investment than air conditioning, which we would use two weeks out of the year. Since both cost about the same, I have to figure out how long it will be until all movies become digital audio. I'd hate to put in A/C, only to discover a month later I need to come up with the bucks to convert my sound system. Unless there is a sudden come-back of the silent movie genre...

Q: Your seats are really uncomfortable.
A: Then get here early and get the sofa, or use one of the movable chairs, or grab a pillow and sit on the floor, or use a folding chair, or haul in your own Laz-E-Boy. We have options. We're good about that. But, you are free to whine, if that helps, too.

Q: I've come in and you have been sold out.
A: Come earlier.

Q: Why don't you ever start at the published show time?
A: Because it's my theater and I'll start when I damn well please—and about a third of our customers show up about five minutes after show time.

Q: When will you have coffee?
A: I'm having some now. Hopefully I'll have some to sell by this winter.

Q: Why don't you serve beer?
A: Because I don't have an Oregon Liquor Control Commission license to sell it. They're really funny about that—serving alcohol without it is generally frowned upon (though, if I served myself enough, I wouldn't worry about it). Besides, most of my customers are crazy enough. Why add alcohol?

Q: Can we bring our own alcohol?
A: If you wanna see me get shut down by the local law. Hell, bring in your own crack. That'll put me outta biz even faster!

Q: You need to do midnight movies.
A: You need to find me a 35mm projectionist with enough experience that I don't have to be here, because I put in long enough hours as it is.

Q: Are you hiring?

A: Depends. I'm broke, so if ya wanna make a living, I ain't it. Also, snack bar help is usually well covered, but I'm always interested in people who have 35mm projector experience (yes, anyone can learn how to thread a projector. But, you need to know what to do when the sound dies and I'm pleasantly smashed at the coast and can't come and fix the problem. That's where the experience comes in), who can think, and who fit into the Avalon atmosphere. Flaky people will be killed the first time the show doesn't run because they over-slept. So, why put me through the trial when no jury would convict me?

Q: How do we contact you?

A: Email me. Don't leave a message at the theater number because I don't listen to them. When we ran the Gay and Lesbian film festival, lots of ignorant, feckless chimps found it necessary to leave rather shitty messages about the festival on the theater number. Since I don't need to listen to that crap, I just don't retrieve the messages from there.

Q: What happened to the Virgin Mary that used to be over the snack bar?

A: She has reappeared near the screen. I took her down after a rather spirited discussion with someone who found her offensive in all her glory over the snack bar. "Disrespectful," was the operative word someone used to describe her display in my theater. And, anyone who knows me knows that I bend over backwards to avoid offending anyone.

Q: Who decorated your theater?

A: Goodwill.

Q: Are you handicapped accessible?

A: We comply with all American with Disabilities Act regulations—and we are even nice about it. We would encourage our wheeled customers to come a wee bit early to get in the auditorium before the show rolls, since the only access to the seating area is past the front of the screen.

Q: Have you started cooking your popcorn in Canola oil yet?

A: Hell no. Watch your fat content at home. We are here for you to forget about life and relax. Part of that is eating fat-filled, flavorful popcorn made the way God intended. Do they sell tofu hot-dogs in Dodger Stadium? If they do, I'll cry.

Q: Why is it I see microphone booms on the top of the frame in movies in your theater?
A: Because we are special. It is an honor bestowed upon only the coolest theaters. And it might also be that I can put in a different framing thing that crops the image (aperture plate), but it would make the movie seem like you're viewing it through a mail-slot. Sometimes I can frame the image down and eliminate most of that, but that often leads to seeing the spotlights normally below the frame. So, I leave it alone and it gives you something to tell your grandchildren about.

Q: Why are your food prices so much higher than Safeway's?
A: Because they sell more of it than I do. You can buy your food at Safeway, or the co-op or wherever and bring it in. That's fine. As long as it doesn't bother you that the profit from the snack bar pays my bills. If you can enjoy a movie while munching on something that doesn't contribute to the sustenance of the Avalon cinema, then have at it. Really. No one will think ill of you.

Q: What's the funniest thing anyone has ever asked you?
A: When we were running the movie "Pecker," a very nice older woman came in and asked, "How long is John Waters' "Pecker?" She had no clue what she had just asked. Fortunately, the half-dozen people in the lobby also figured she hadn't grokked what had just come outta her mouth. I looked at her and said, "The movie is 88 minutes long." She thanked me and left. As soon as she was clear of the door, everyone lost it. I'm sure she sat bolt upright at 3 a.m. realizing what she had asked. And no, I have no idea how long John Waters'...

Q: The most annoying question?
A: "What do you do for your day job?" has to be the most frequent question that comes under the heading of: Slap Magnet. During the day I book movies, do box office reports, clean and lubricate projectors, clean up the auditorium, scrub the toilets, get supplies, and answer stupid questions.

Good News And Bad News (January 1999)

Good News: We are now using a professional national booker to get movies for the Avalon Cinema.

Bad News: We have to raise the admission to $5.50 for General Admission after January 8, 1999.

Good News: This should be the last rate hike for a spell.

Bad News: I have nothing to base that statement upon.

Good News: We are keeping Senior and Cheap Nite rates the same.

Bad News: The snack bar prices will have to go up, too.

Good News: You can bitch to the guy who's doing this. Not Paul's daughter.

Bad News: He won't be too receptive since the last price change was over a year ago—and admission price went *down* a buck that time.

Good News: The pink Gift Certificates will be honored for the complete $5.50 admission (or whatever they were issued for) after the 8th. Right up until we say otherwise.

Bad News: The yellow ones will not. They will be worth only their issued price after the 8th.

Good News: Many of our programs will be double features. (That's one admission for two flicks!)

Bad News: You will have to bring a friend, since soaking in all that good film for so long is not advised as a solo activity.

Good News: We're still a great deal.

More Good News:

It's people like you that keep us open. Thanks!

Even More Good News:

It just keeps getting better, and this new booker should make that even truer!

FAQs for the Darkside Cinema (April 2006)

Time for a little Q&A. First the As:

1) We don't control the surround sound. If you are not hearing them, it's because there is not a surround track in the sound track. The processor in the booth decides if we have surround or not. We do not turn it off or on. We do not turn it up or down. This expensive piece of equipment we have in the projection booth does all that. We played NEIL YOUNG: HEART OF GOLD in two auditoriums. Neither had a huge amount of surround sound.

2) Go play on the freeway.

3) Guess what? That *is* the sound system from the Avalon.

4) Me, too. Hit eBay.

5) Waaaah.

6) Not without a note from my wife.

7) Not without a notarized note from my wife.

8) $10 is my limit. Just like in Vegas.

9) "Let go of my ears. I know what I'm doing."

10) Because the Internet porn and morphine ain't doin' it for me anymore.

And now, the Qs:

1) Why did you turn off the surround sound?

2) When will the Avalon be open again?

3) The sound system at the Avalon was way better than the one you have in auditorium two.

4) I *really* like THE WORLD'S FASTEST INDIAN poster.

5) I don't like your show times.

6) Can I talk to you about a business idea I have?

7) I'd like to see how you look without that Avalon Cinema T-shirt on, big boy.

8) How much would you gamble someone will be offended by these Q&As?

9) What are you likely to hear through the collection department door of any movie company?

10) Why did you install a video surveillance system?

....

There are times I reread the old FAQs and wonder how people put up with my irascibility, which often moved into rudeness. It wasn't just me hiding behind the doors or the Internet. I was this rude in person, too. I suspect there are very few towns in the country that would put up with someone like me. I'm very fortunate to be in Corvallis, Oregon. As always, thanks for supporting us. We will never take you for granted. We know it is *you* who makes independent cinema in Corvallis what it is. Thanks!

Acknowledgments

There are many people who helped along this journey. The first to be recognized is my partner and wife, Lainie. I spread my words out in front of her and she mixes and matches them so they become coherent. Her gift for flavor and flow of language makes my ponderous prose into something people will read. She is careful about unfolding the adolescent double entendre and trying to divine what it was I was really trying to say—never taking the liberty of just using her own words.

Many of you have the grace and humor to allow me to tell stories about our foibles together. In this, there is a trust that I will never compromise—and a kindness that will not be diminished by the years.

Nothing happens unless people buy tickets. Here's to those who walk through the doors every week, with money in their hands and charity in their hearts. They endure the cataclysmic humor of mechanical chance and the unforeseen events that would send the less hearty screaming out the door. And then come back again the next week. I sincerely hope my affection and gratitude can be easily seen through the transparence of my often less-than-garrulous façade.

So many of us count on the kindness and attention of the people who support us when the usual channels become strained. They have the propriety to avert their eyes when in public so as not to betray a connection, and are quick to find a slot of time when the moments of health seem a little too far apart. I suspect very little in this city happens without their help.